Copyright © 2025 Stand Again

All rights reserved.

No part of this publication may be reproduced, stored in a retrieval system, or transmitted in any form or by any means - electronic, mechanical, photocopying, recording, or otherwise - without prior written permission from the author, except for brief quotations used in reviews or critical articles.

Stand Again is a registered business operating under ABN 75 563 353 277.

www.standagain.com.au

Disclaimer

This guide is based on lived experience, independent research, and insights drawn from recovery work with survivors of abuse. It is intended for educational and self-reflective purposes only. It is not a substitute for professional mental health care, diagnosis, or treatment.

Some of the topics discussed may bring up strong emotions or memories. If you feel overwhelmed at any point, pause your reading and consider reaching out to a trusted friend, counsellor, or helpline. You are the best judge of your own readiness and pace.

Any strategies, approaches, or examples included here are suggestions, not prescriptions. Every survivor's journey is unique - what works for one person may not work for another. Take what serves you, adapt it to your needs, and leave the rest.

If you are currently in danger or experiencing distress, please seek immediate support from a qualified professional or crisis service in your area.

Table of Contents

INTRODUCTION 4
- It Happens to Even the Best of Men 5
- How to Use This Book 8
- A Note to Clinicians 10

PART ONE: UNDERSTANDING WHAT'S HAPPENING 13
- Chapter 1: What You're Witnessing 14
- Chapter 2: The Male Experience 24

PART TWO: YOUR ROLE 31
- Chapter 3: The Truth About Change 32
- Chapter 4: Leaving the Light On 44

PART THREE: BUILDING A UNIFIED FAMILY FRONT 50
- Chapter 5: Working Together 51
- Chapter 6: Sustaining Yourself 61

PART FOUR: THE JOURNEY 70
- Understanding the Stages 71
- Chapter 7: Stage One - Deep in the System 72
- Chapter 8: Stage Two - Cracks Forming 91
- Chapter 9: Stage Three - Crisis Point 98
- Chapter 10: Stage Four - Early Exit 105
- Chapter 11: Stage Five - Reconstruction 114

PART FIVE: SAFETY AND THE ABUSER 122
Chapter 12: Dealing With Her 123

PART SIX: SPECIFIC COMPLICATIONS 138
Chapter 13: Complications 139

PART SEVEN: SPECIFIC RELATIONSHIPS 155
Chapter 14: If You Are 156

PART EIGHT: THE LONG VIEW 169
Chapter 15: Living With Uncertainty 170
Conclusion 178

APPENDIX 179
Appendix A: Quick Reference 180
Appendix B: Resources 183
Acknowledgments 186

INTRODUCTION

It Happens to Even the Best of Men

Coercive control happens to men. This is a statement that shouldn't require defence, yet it does. The overwhelming majority of resources, services, and public conversation about domestic abuse centres on women as victims and men as perpetrators. This framing reflects a genuine reality for many people, but it also renders invisible the significant number of men who experience the same patterns of psychological manipulation, isolation, and control.

This book exists because families of male victims have almost nowhere to turn. When a parent watches their son disappear into a relationship that is clearly destroying him, when siblings see their brother transformed into someone they no longer recognise, when friends witness a man they've known for decades become isolated, anxious, and diminished, they search for guidance and find almost nothing.

And because men experience coercive control differently because they are men. The tactics used against them exploit masculine identity specifically. The barriers to recognition and help-seeking are shaped by cultural expectations of what men should be. The systems that should help them often treat them as the threat rather than the victim. And the shame that keeps them trapped operates through beliefs about masculinity, competence, and self-reliance that must be understood if families are to reach them.

None of this diminishes the experience of female victims. Abuse is abuse. But helping someone requires understanding the specific shape of their prison, and men's prisons are built with particular walls that this book will help you see.

If you're reading this book, someone you love is in this kind of trouble right now.

You are watching someone you love disappear, and you don't know how to stop it. And you deserve guidance that takes your specific situation seriously.

Perhaps it started with small changes. He stopped calling as often. Family gatherings became complicated negotiations. His opinions began sounding

like someone else's words. Or perhaps it was sudden and dramatic: he announced he was cutting off contact, accused you of things that made no sense, defended behaviour that the person you knew would never have tolerated.

You have probably tried to help. You may have tried to point out what you see, to reason with him, to present evidence, to issue ultimatums. And you have likely discovered that none of it works. In fact, much of it seems to make things worse.

I wrote this book because I have lived what your loved one is living.

For a decade, I was caught in a relationship that dismantled me piece by piece while I insisted everything was fine. I pushed away family members who tried to express concern. I defended my partner against any suggestion that something was wrong. I made excuses, rationalised, and genuinely believed I was in a loving relationship that others simply didn't understand.

I also know what it took for me to finally see clearly. It wasn't a dramatic intervention or an ultimatum from my family. The people who ultimately helped me were those who stayed present without pushing, who kept the door open without trying to drag me through it, who maintained connection even when I gave them every reason to walk away.

Alongside this book sits the rest of the Stand Again work. A broader framework to make sense of patterns like the one you are seeing now. *The Blueprint of Family Violence Against Men* www.standagain.com.au maps out the main tactics used against men in abusive relationships. The TTI model *[Tactic, Trigger, Impact]* helps survivors, families and clinicians understand how specific behaviours trigger particular reactions and leave lasting psychological marks.

You do not need to study those frameworks to use this book. Everything you need to support your son, brother, or friend is contained here. But if, at any point, you want a more detailed map of the patterns you're witnessing, those resources are there for you.

There is also a companion book that focuses specifically on what happens after a man leaves an abusive relationship and begins trying to reconnect with his own emotional life. It is called *Reconnecting With Your Feelings After*

Abuse. If your loved one does eventually reach the point of separation, that book may help you understand why he finds it so hard to feel present, safe, or emotionally available - even when the abuse has stopped.

This book is the resource I wish my own family had possessed. It is written from lived experience of coercive control and from my time working with men in these situations and the families who love them. It will not give you a magic solution, because there isn't one. What it will give you is:

- Understanding of what is actually happening
- Clarity about what helps and what harms
- A framework for staying connected to someone who has been disconnected from those that care about him
- Guidance for each stage of the journey

For more practical tools including exit planning templates, visit www.standagain.com.au

The core approach in this book is called 'leaving the light on.' You cannot force him out.

You can, however, do far more than simply wait and watch. You can understand the mechanisms that trap him. Learn what reaches him and what pushes him further away. You can become the person he turns to when the cracks begin to form. You can position yourself to matter at the moments that matter most. This book shows you how.

What you are attempting is not hopeless. People do escape coercive control. Families do reunite. But the path is longer and less direct than you want it to be, and success requires understanding dynamics that are deeply counterintuitive.

I'm here because my family refused to give up on me. This book is my attempt to help you do the same for your son, your brother, or your friend. And before you launch into it, please know:

You did not cause this. You cannot control it. But you are not powerless.

How to Use This Book

This book is designed to be read in full first, then used as an ongoing reference as your situation evolves. Understanding the complete picture before taking action will help you avoid well-intentioned mistakes that can set back your efforts significantly.

For brevity and simplicity only, the language may default to a parent and son relationship. The lessons and approaches however, are applicable for parents, siblings, and friends. Part Seven explores these nuances further.

The book is organised into eight parts:

- **Part One: Understanding What's Happening** explains the nature of coercive control, why your son cannot see his situation clearly, and why men face particular barriers to recognition and escape.

- **Part Two: Your Role** addresses what you can and cannot do, helping you develop a sustainable posture of active patience rather than either passive acceptance or counterproductive intervention.

- **Part Three: Building a Unified Family Front** covers the practical work of aligning family members around a shared approach and sustaining yourselves emotionally through what may be a lengthy process.

- **Part Four: The Journey** walks through the five stages your son may pass through from deep entrapment to eventual freedom, with specific guidance for each stage.

- **Part Five: Safety and the Abuser** addresses how to handle contact with your son's partner, protect your communications, and manage safety concerns.

- **Part Six: Specific Complications** covers particular circumstances that may apply to your situation: children, pregnancy, addiction, financial dependence, and other factors.

- **Part Seven: Specific Relationships** offers tailored guidance based on your relationship to the victim such as parent, sibling, or friend.

- **Part Eight: The Long View** addresses the realities of extended timelines, including what to do if he never leaves and how to maintain hope without destroying yourself.

If you're in crisis, start with the stage that matches where he is now. If you have time, the earlier sections will help everything else make more sense.

A Note to Clinicians

If you are a therapist, counsellor, social worker, or other professional working with families of male abuse victims, this book offers a framework that complements clinical practice. Several dimensions warrant particular attention.

The approach here is informed by:

- Research on high-control groups and cult dynamics
- The transtheoretical model of change (stages of change)
- Motivational interviewing principles
- Direct work with male victims and their families

Regarding male victims:

- **Men rarely identify as victims** and may never use this language even when describing clear abuse. Assessment instruments developed for female victims may miss male victimisation patterns.

- **Shame operates as a particularly powerful silencing mechanism** for men, compounding the effects of the abuse itself. The intersection of victimisation with masculine identity creates psychological dynamics that differ from those typically described in domestic abuse literature.

- **Men in coercive control situations commonly present with symptoms that mask** underlying relationship abuse: workplace stress, generalised anxiety, depression, substance use, or somatic complaints. Direct questioning about relationship dynamics may be less effective than creating space for indirect disclosure.

One of the recurrent challenges in this space is distinguishing male victims from mutual conflict or covert aggression.

Men who have been subjected to coercive control often present with flat affect, tightly managed emotional expression, and a strong impulse to protect their partner's image. They may minimise their own distress, emphasise their partner's past trauma, or present themselves as the one who "loses control" because they occasionally react under extreme provocation. **Without a clear framework, it is easy to misread these presentations and assume that he is the primary problem.**

A related bias compounds this problem. Men's emotional displays are judged more harshly than women's. Men are expected to remain stoic at all times, showing no anger, no frustration, no visible distress. This expectation is so deeply embedded in cultural expectations that even clinicians can sometimes carry it. When a woman displays outward emotion it can sometimes read as passion or be dismissed as justifiable even if it is not. When a man does the same, it reads as aggression, danger, potential violence, or even as though it is fabricated to curry favour.

This means that when a male victim presents with any evidence of emotional outbursts or breakdowns, the emotional display often becomes the entire clinical focus. He is quickly categorised as a perpetrator, as mutually abusive, or even as manipulative for showing tears or breaking down in distress, rather than as a man who has been pushed past breaking point by sustained psychological abuse. His reactive moments eclipse her months or years of provocation.

Clinicians working with men in these situations must hold this bias in conscious awareness. The question is not simply "has he ever lost control?" The question is "what was happening to him when he did?"

The Stand Again Blueprint of Family Violence Against Men and the TTI model (Tactic, Trigger, Impact) are designed to assist with this differentiation.

- **The Blueprint** outlines the core tactics most commonly used against men across psychological, emotional, financial, and parental domains.

- **The TTI model** helps clinicians map specific incidents to the underlying tactic, the internal trigger it hits in the man, and the behavioural or emotional impact that follows.

Together, they provide a structured way of understanding patterns that might otherwise be dismissed as "just relationship issues" or misattributed as mutual volatility. These frameworks are available on the Stand Again website.

These tools are not intended to replace your clinical judgement. They are scaffolding. They offer a way to hold in mind that a man who looks calm, vague, compliant, or self-blaming may be navigating a highly controlled environment and a deep conflict between his sense of masculine identity and his lived experience of being harmed.

Regarding families:

- **Family members of male victims often encounter scepticism** from professionals. Validating their observations while providing psychoeducation about coercive control patterns serves both the family and, ultimately, the victim.

- **Families benefit from explicit permission to prioritise their own wellbeing** alongside their efforts to help. The natural tendency is complete self-sacrifice, which leads to burnout before the often-lengthy process completes.

- **Psychoeducation about stages of change**, reactance, and the counterproductive nature of direct intervention helps families channel their energy more effectively.

- **Families benefit from validation that their observations are real**, education about dynamics, coaching on communication approaches, and help managing their own emotional responses. They often need permission to step back from rescue attempts that aren't working.

- **Family members may present with symptoms** similar to those of abuse victims themselves: hypervigilance, rumination, anticipatory anxiety, and complicated grief for a relationship that hasn't ended but has fundamentally changed.

This book provides families with a framework they can reference between sessions and a vocabulary for discussing their situation. It is not a substitute for clinical support, particularly when family members are experiencing significant psychological distress or when safety concerns exist.

Stand Again offers coaching for clinicians.

Details at **www.standagain.com.au**

PART ONE: UNDERSTANDING WHAT'S HAPPENING

Chapter 1: What You're Witnessing

Something is deeply wrong. You can feel it even when you can't fully articulate what you're seeing. This chapter explains the nature of what your son is experiencing and why it remains invisible to him.

This Isn't Your Fault

Before we go any further, you need to hear something clearly: you did not cause this, you cannot control it, and you cannot cure it through sheer force of love or willpower.

The questions that keep you awake at night.

"What did I miss?"

"Should I have raised him differently?"

"Why didn't I see this sooner?"

"Why can't I fix this?"

These questions are natural. They're also based on a false premise. Coercive control is not something that happens to people because of childhood deficits or family failures. Intelligent, emotionally healthy people from loving homes fall victim to abusive partners. The qualities that made your son a good person - his loyalty, his willingness to see the best in others, his commitment to making relationships work - are precisely the qualities that skilled abusers exploit.

You are also not responsible for the limits of your power here. A parent's instinct is to protect their child from harm, and the inability to do so triggers profound feelings of failure. But coercive control creates conditions specifically designed to prevent outside intervention. The isolation, the reality distortion, the way your son now defends his abuser - these are features of the abuse, not signs that you've failed to love him enough.

Blaming yourself accomplishes nothing except depleting the emotional resources you will need for the long road ahead. Your son needs you present and capable, not destroyed by guilt over circumstances you did not create and cannot control.

What you can do, and what this book will help you do, is position yourself strategically to be there when he's ready. That is real love, and it is enough.

What Coercive Control Is

When most people think of domestic abuse, they picture physical violence: bruises, broken bones, visible injuries. The most devastating form of intimate partner abuse, however, leaves no marks on the body. Coercive control is a pattern of behaviour that strips away a person's autonomy, independence, and sense of self through non-violent means that are often invisible to outsiders and even to the victim.

The term was developed by researcher Evan Stark, who observed that many victims of domestic abuse described their experience as being similar to prisoners of war or hostages. This was not because of physical violence. It was because of the psychological environment their partner had constructed. Coercive control operates through restriction, surveillance, humiliation, and manipulation. Physical force may also be present, though it is not the primary mechanism.

Understanding coercive control requires understanding four interconnected domains of influence. These domains form a comprehensive framework. Each reinforces the others, creating a closed system that becomes increasingly difficult to escape.

The Four Domains of Coercive Control

Domain	How It Operates
Behaviour Control	Dictating where he can go, who he can see, how he spends his time and money. Creating rules that are impossible to follow consistently, ensuring he is always in violation of some expectation. Using children, finances, or housing as leverage to enforce compliance.
Information Control	Monitoring communications, isolating him from friends and family who might offer outside perspective, creating a distorted narrative about reality that he has no way to fact-check. Controlling what information enters the relationship and how it is interpreted.
Thought Control	Installing her framework for interpreting reality, making him doubt his own perceptions and memories, framing her needs and interpretations as objectively correct while his are flawed. Training him to view the relationship through her lens rather than trusting his own judgment.
Emotional Control	Manufacturing fear, obligation, and guilt to maintain compliance. Creating emotional dependency through intermittent reinforcement: unpredictable cycles of warmth and coldness, approval and criticism. Making his emotional stability dependent on her approval, which is always conditional and can be withdrawn at any moment.

These tactics rarely appear suddenly or obviously. They emerge gradually, each step seeming reasonable in context. By the time the pattern becomes clear to an outsider, the person inside it has already been trained to interpret these behaviours as normal aspects of their relationship or as responses to their own failures.

The cumulative effect is the creation of a private reality that only the two of them occupy. A reality in which her demands are reasonable, his needs are excessive, her anger is justified, and his pain is evidence of his inadequacy. From inside this reality, outside perspectives appear uninformed at best, hostile at worst.

This is why your son defends her. This is why he dismisses your concerns. He is not choosing her over you; he is operating within a reality that has been carefully constructed to make your perspective seem wrong.

Why He Can't See It

If what you're reading about coercive control seems obvious, you may wonder why your son, intelligent and capable as he is, cannot see what seems clear to you. His blindness is not stupidity or weakness. It is the predictable result of specific psychological mechanisms that operate on everyone, regardless of intelligence or education.

How the Relationship Was Formed

Understanding how your son entered this relationship can help you make sense of what you're witnessing. Abusive relationships typically form through one of four patterns:

- The first is the **entrapment fantasy**. She swept him off his feet. Love bombing, intense connection, the sense that he had finally found someone who truly understood him. The fairy tale became a cage so gradually he never saw the walls going up.

- The second is the **rescuer turned ruled**. He entered the relationship as her saviour. She needed him. She was vulnerable, struggling, and he could help. Somewhere along the way, the dynamic flipped. Now he cannot leave someone who "needs" him, even as she controls him.

- The third is called the **"I told you so" confession**. From the beginning she openly advertises her harshness and unrealistic expectations. "I'm the jealous type", "My love language is insults." It sounds like brutal honesty, but it's actually a setup. When the abuse does arrives, she doesn't deny it. She tells him she warned him. That he "knew what he signed up for, so accept her for who she is".

- The fourth is the **chaos trap**. The relationship has always been crisis. Drama, intensity, problems that demand his attention. He has never had space to think clearly because there is always something urgent happening. The chaos itself keeps him reactive and unable to step back.

Different men fall through different doors. Understanding which door your son entered helps explain his particular shame, what dimension of tactics she will deploy, and what he will need to process and repair when he eventually emerges.

For deeper exploration of these patterns, and how they evolve within an abusive dynamic, see the Stand Again YouTube channel.

The Gradual Shift

Coercive control never begins with its full intensity. The early relationship likely felt wonderful. Exciting, intimate, perhaps the most connected he has ever felt with anyone. The concerning behaviours emerged incrementally, each one small enough to rationalise, each escalation explicable by circumstances that seemed to justify it.

This is the boiling frog phenomenon. If you drop a frog into boiling water, it will immediately jump out. But if you place it in cool water and heat it gradually, the frog will remain until it's too late. Your son entered a relationship that felt safe and loving. Each adjustment he made was minor. The person he is today (isolated, defensive, exhausted) is the result of hundreds of small adaptations, none of which individually seemed alarming.

You, viewing from outside, see the dramatic transformation. You remember who he was before. He does not have this perspective. He experiences only the continuous present, each day connected to the day before it in a chain of small, explicable adjustments.

Cognitive Dissonance

Your son holds two contradictory beliefs that cannot both be true: "I am an intelligent, capable person who makes good decisions" and "I am in a relationship that is destroying me." The psychological discomfort of holding these contradictory beliefs is profound. This discomfort is called cognitive dissonance. And the mind will do remarkable things to resolve it.

The easiest resolution is to reject the second belief. If his relationship is actually fine, if the problems are either exaggerated by others or caused by his own failures, then there is no contradiction. He remains intelligent and capable; he simply has a partner who challenges him to grow. This interpretation allows him to maintain his self-image and avoid the devastating conclusion that he has been victimised.

Accepting that he is in an abusive relationship would require a fundamental reconstruction of his understanding of himself, his partner, and his life. It is psychologically easier to construct elaborate explanations for why everything is actually fine.

The Collapse of the Outside View

To recognise abuse, one must be able to step outside the abuser's framework and evaluate the relationship by external standards. Isolation has removed most external reference points. His friends have drifted away. He may have limited contact with colleagues. You, his family, are likely framed as hostile to the relationship and therefore unreliable narrators.

The information environment he inhabits is dominated by her interpretations. She explains events. She frames conflicts. She defines what constitutes reasonable expectations and appropriate responses. Without access to external perspectives, he lacks the data needed to question her version of reality.

His previous understanding of what healthy relationships look like has been gradually replaced with her framework. The baseline has shifted. Things that would once have seemed alarming now seem normal because they have become normal for him, in this relationship, in this carefully controlled environment.

Trauma Bonding

The intermittent reinforcement pattern inherent in abusive relationships creates powerful biochemical bonds. When stress and relief cycle unpredictably, when affection and criticism alternate in ways he cannot anticipate or control, the brain responds by forming intense attachments to the source of both pain and comfort.

This is the same mechanism that makes gambling addictive. The unpredictability of reward strengthens rather than weakens the behaviour. The moments when she is loving and kind feel more precious and more meaningful because they are surrounded by uncertainty. He chases those moments, working harder and harder to produce them, not recognising that their scarcity is manufactured rather than earned.

The bond he feels toward her is genuine, neurologically indistinguishable from healthy attachment. When you criticise her, you are attacking someone he genuinely loves. Someone his brain has learned to associate with survival itself.

The Self That Copes

The son you're seeing now is not entirely the son you raised. In response to the demands of his environment, he has developed an adapted self. A version of himself optimised for survival within the relationship. This adapted self minimises conflict, prioritises her needs, and interprets events in ways that maintain the peace.

His authentic self has been pushed underground. The one who had independent preferences, who might have challenged her demands, who once had relationships and interests outside of her. It is not destroyed. It is simply not currently in control. The adapted self runs interference, protecting him from the consequences of authentic expression within a relationship that punishes authenticity.

When you talk to him now, you are often talking to the adapted self. This self has been trained to defend the relationship, to maintain the narrative that everything is fine, and to distance himself from anyone who threatens the carefully maintained equilibrium. This is why he sometimes seems like a stranger. In a very real sense, you are not speaking to all of him.

What If You're Wrong?

Before you commit to understanding your son's situation as coercive control, it's worth pausing on an uncomfortable question: what if you're misreading things?

This question is not a betrayal of your instincts. It's due diligence. The approaches in this book are patient, non-interventionist, and designed for situations involving genuine abuse. They would be counterproductive if applied to a relationship that is merely difficult or different from what you expected.

Misdiagnosis hurts everyone: you, because you exhaust yourself addressing the wrong problem; your son, because you treat him as a victim when he isn't; and your relationship, because your stance creates unnecessary distance.

Reality-Checking Your Perception

Ask yourself honestly:

- **Would any partner have triggered your concern?** Some parents struggle with their child's partner regardless of who that partner is. If your son's previous relationships also seemed problematic to you, or if you find yourself critical of other family members' partners, your concern may reflect your difficulty with his independence rather than genuine problems with this relationship.

- **Is your concern about her, or about the relationship not meeting your expectations?** Different is not dangerous. His relationship may look nothing like yours, involve dynamics you find uncomfortable, or follow patterns you wouldn't choose. None of this is abuse.

- **Are the changes in him negative, or just different?** People change in relationships. Sometimes they become quieter, more domestic, less available to their parents. This is normal adult development, not evidence of control.

- **Could his distance from you reflect relationship issues with you rather than control by her?** If he's pulling away from family, consider whether family dynamics are part of the reason. Sometimes adult children need distance from their families of origin. This can be healthy.

- **Have you spoken to anyone outside the family?** Friends, a therapist, someone with distance from the situation - what do they see? Multiple independent sources of concern are more credible than family consensus, which can reflect shared biases.

What Healthy Relationship Friction Looks Like

All relationships involve some adjustment, some conflict, some distance from families of origin. What distinguishes normal relationship friction from coercive control:

- **Reciprocity.** In healthy relationships, both partners make adjustments. He may see less of his family, but so may she. Both make space for each other's needs. In coercive control, adjustment flows in one direction.

- **He still seems like himself.** Partners influence each other, but the core self remains. If he has new interests, that's influence. If he seems to have lost his personality, that's something else.

- **He can disagree with her.** In healthy relationships, partners can express different opinions without fear. If he never disagrees with her, always defers to her, seems anxious about contradicting her, then that's a warning sign.

- **He has freedom.** He can make plans, see friends, make decisions without checking with her first. He has space for a life outside the relationship.

- **The relationship makes him happier.** Even when relationships involve less time with family, they should add to life satisfaction. If he seems diminished rather than enriched, something is wrong.

If You're Uncertain

Uncertainty is okay. You don't need to be certain to act appropriately.

The approach this book recommends (warm presence, unconditional availability, non-judgmental connection) is appropriate even if you're wrong about the abuse. Maintaining good relationship with your adult child is healthy regardless of his relationship status.

What's inappropriate, if you're wrong: treating him as a victim who needs rescuing, treating her as an enemy to be opposed, treating the relationship as a problem to be solved. These stances damage relationships with adult children whether or not abuse is present.

If you're uncertain, proceed with the connection-focused elements of this book while holding your interpretation loosely. Watch. Wait. Remain open to being wrong.

Chapter 2: The Male Experience

Men experience coercive control with particular dimensions that generic abuse resources rarely address. Understanding these specific vulnerabilities helps explain what you're witnessing and what your son is facing.

Why Men Are Particularly Vulnerable

Most mainstream descriptions of abuse are written with women in mind. They are accurate for many situations. They also leave men out of the picture almost completely. When families search for answers, they often try to fit what they are seeing into those descriptions and come away confused. Their son does not look like the victims they have been taught to imagine. He may seem composed when they are distressed, stubborn when they are scared, defensive when they are vulnerable.

Seen through a male lens, these reactions make sense. Men are taught to be reliable, self-contained, and in control. They are rewarded for shouldering burdens quietly and criticised when they show weakness. Coercive partners do not fight that conditioning; they lean into it. They use it. Understanding how masculine identity is being played with and turned against him will help you make sense of why your son behaves as he does, and why simple appeals to "just leave" or "see what she's doing" rarely land.

The reality is, the tactics of coercive control are largely universal, but they land differently on male victims because of the cultural expectations that shape masculine identity. The very qualities that society celebrates in men, such as reliability, stoicism, competence, commitment to their word, all become vulnerabilities that skilled abusers exploit.

How Masculine Identity Creates Vulnerability

Masculine Quality	How It Becomes Weaponised
Provider Identity	His sense of responsibility for family welfare is used to justify overwork, financial control, and guilt when he cannot meet ever-escalating demands. "A real man provides" becomes a lever to extract more while making him feel he is failing.
Commitment to His Word	The masculine value of keeping promises is exploited to enforce compliance. Past agreements are weaponised: "You said you would..." "You promised..." His integrity is used against him.
Stoicism	His socialisation to suppress emotional expression means he absorbs distress without outlets. He doesn't complain, doesn't seek help, doesn't name what's happening, because men are supposed to handle things themselves.
Problem-Solver Role	His belief that he should be able to fix any situation keeps him engaged long past the point of reason. If he were just smarter, more patient, better, then he could solve this. Leaving feels like failure.
Protector Role	His impulse to protect is turned inward: he protects her reputation, her feelings, her version of events. He also protects himself from the shame of admitting he's being harmed by someone he's supposed to protect himself from.
Sexual Adequacy	His sexual performance and desirability may be attacked, weaponised, or used as a reward system. Intimacy becomes transactional, conditional, and fraught with anxiety about adequacy.

Masculine Quality	How It Becomes Weaponised
Peacekeeper Role	The cultural script of "happy wife, happy life" teaches men that relationship harmony is their job to maintain. His role is to absorb her moods, manage her emotions, and keep the peace at any cost. When conflict arises, he assumes it is his failure. She reinforces this: if he were a better partner, she would not be upset. He works harder to keep her happy, which means working harder to erase himself.
Self-Reliance	The expectation that men should handle their own problems prevents him from seeking support. Reaching out for help would mean admitting he cannot cope. An admission that feels like failure of masculinity itself.

The particular cruelty of these dynamics is that they create self-sealing traps. The more he tries to be a "good man" by the traditional definitions he was raised with, the more material she has to exploit. **His virtues become chains.**

The Double Bind of Disclosure

Beyond the exploitation of masculine identity within the relationship, men face additional barriers when considering disclosure to the outside world. The word "victim" is deeply incompatible with masculine identity. Men are supposed to be strong, capable, in control. Victimhood implies weakness, vulnerability, helplessness. Everything masculinity is defined against.

This creates a double bind. To get help, he must identify as a victim. But identifying as a victim threatens his sense of himself as a man. Many men resolve this by simply refusing to frame their experience in these terms, even internally. They may acknowledge that their relationship is difficult, stressful, or draining. They stop short of terminology that would require seeing themselves as abused.

Your son may never use the word "abuse" to describe his situation. He may never call himself a victim. This does not mean he does not know something is wrong. It means he lacks a framework that allows him to name it while maintaining his sense of masculine identity.

The Fear of Not Being Believed

Men who have disclosed abuse often report being met with disbelief, minimisation, or mockery – even from psychologists. Friends may respond with jokes. Professionals may be dismissive. The cultural narrative that positions men as perpetrators and women as victims makes it difficult for people to recognise female-to-male abuse even when presented with clear evidence.

Your son has likely absorbed these expectations. He anticipates that disclosure will not lead to support but to scepticism or ridicule. Why would he risk the shame of reaching out if he expects to be told he's exaggerating, that he should man up, or that if he's really being mistreated he should simply leave?

He may also fear being seen as the aggressor. Men who report domestic abuse are sometimes arrested themselves. The assumption that men are dangerous and women are vulnerable can lead police, courts, and social services to misidentify him as the perpetrator. This is not paranoia; it is a documented pattern that men in his situation learn to fear.

The Invisible Crisis

Cultural stigma, internalised shame, anticipated disbelief, and absence of services combine to create a situation where male victims often suffer in complete silence. Female victims face serious barriers. But they do at least have a cultural narrative that acknowledges their existence. Male victims often lack even the language to describe what is happening to them – which is why Stand Again created the *Blueprint of Family Violence Against Men*, to provide language where there is none.

Your son may be living in a crisis that nobody else can see. He may be drowning in plain sight, surrounded by people who assume that because he is a man, he cannot be drowning. He may have tried to signal distress in ways

that were not recognised because they did not match the expected pattern of how victims behave.

Understanding these specific dynamics helps explain why he seems unable to take steps that appear obvious from outside. It is not that he lacks the intelligence or the strength. It is that every path forward requires confronting barriers (internal and external) that feel insurmountable.

Why Leaving Feels Impossible

From outside the relationship, leaving may seem straightforward: recognise that you are being abused, pack your things, and go. From inside, the path is obstructed by barriers that feel insurmountable. This is not because your son is weak. Coercive control is specifically designed to make leaving feel impossible.

The Barriers He Faces

- **He does not fully recognise the situation.** As discussed above, the gradual nature of coercive control, combined with cognitive dissonance, trauma bonding, and the adapted self, means he may genuinely not understand that he is being abused. You cannot leave something you do not believe exists.

- **He is protecting the relationship, not himself.** His adapted self is oriented toward maintaining the relationship, not toward his own wellbeing. The thought of leaving triggers the trauma bond: the intense attachment that has formed precisely because of the intermittent reinforcement pattern. Leaving feels less like escape and more like losing part of himself.

- **He fears what happens after.** Abusers often make clear, explicitly or implicitly, the consequences of leaving: custody battles, false accusations, financial ruin, social destruction. She may have threatened to harm herself if he leaves. He may believe she is unstable enough to follow through. The period immediately after leaving is statistically the most dangerous time for abuse victims, and he may sense this even without the statistics.

- **The children.** If children are involved, he faces the agonising calculation of whether they are better off with him inside the relationship or with him outside it but with reduced access. He may correctly fear that family courts will favour her, that she will use the children as weapons, or that leaving will harm them more than staying. He stays to protect them, even as staying destroys him.

- **He has nowhere to go.** The resources available for women leaving abusive relationships (refuges, emergency housing, domestic violence services) barely exist for men. He may know, correctly, that if he leaves he will have nowhere to stay. She may control the finances, making practical departure logistically difficult.

- **Shame keeps him silent.** Asking for help requires admitting to a situation that feels deeply shameful. He may prefer suffering in silence to experiencing the humiliation of revealing what his life has become. Particularly to you, his family, whose respect and admiration he does not want to lose.

- **He fears the system.** He may have witnessed or heard about men who tried to leave and were accused of being abusers themselves. He may fear that calling police or seeking legal help will result in his own arrest or in court proceedings that destroy him. The system, as he understands it, is not designed to help people like him.

- **He still believes he can fix it.** The problem-solver mentality keeps him engaged. If he could just find the right approach, say the right things, be better. Surely he could turn this around. Leaving feels like giving up, and giving up is not something he does.

These barriers interact and reinforce each other. The shame prevents him from seeking information that might help him recognise the abuse. The lack of recognition prevents him from making a plan. The absence of a plan makes leaving feel chaotic and dangerous. The danger reinforces staying. The staying deepens the entrapment.

Understanding why leaving feels impossible should not lead to hopelessness. People do leave. Your son can leave. Understanding these barriers helps explain why "just leave" is not helpful advice, and why the path forward requires something more sophisticated than appeals to his rationality.

And when someone asks you why he does not just leave, these barriers are your answer. Cognitive dissonance, trauma bonding, loss of agency, psychological destabilisation, and cultural disbelief all operate beneath conscious awareness. He is not choosing to stay the way someone chooses a restaurant. He is trapped by psychological architecture designed to make leaving unthinkable.

For a deeper breakdown of these mechanisms, see the Stand Again YouTube channel.

KEY TAKEAWAYS:

- **YOUR SON IS TRAPPED IN A CAREFULLY CONSTRUCTED REALITY THAT PREVENTS HIM FROM SEEING HIS SITUATION CLEARLY.**

- **THE DYNAMICS KEEPING HIM IN PLACE ARE PSYCHOLOGICAL AND PRACTICAL, NOT CHARACTER FLAWS. UNDERSTANDING THIS IS THE FOUNDATION FOR EVERYTHING THAT FOLLOWS:**

- **YOU CANNOT ARGUE HIM OUT OF A PRISON HE DOESN'T KNOW HE'S IN.**

- **BUT YOU CAN POSITION YOURSELF TO BE THERE WHEN HIS OWN RECOGNITION BEGINS TO EMERGE.**

PART TWO: YOUR ROLE

Chapter 3: The Truth About Change

You want to help him. Every instinct tells you to act, to intervene, to do something that will break through and bring him back. This chapter explains why most interventions fail, what actually creates the conditions for change, and how to channel your love into approaches that might actually work.

What Eventually Breaks Control

People do escape coercive control. Relationships that seemed permanent do end. Men who appeared completely lost do find their way back. Understanding what actually enables this provides the foundation for everything else this book will ask you to do.

The uncomfortable truth is that external pressure rarely breaks coercive control. Ultimatums, interventions, dramatic confrontations. These approaches feel powerful because they allow you to express the urgency you feel. They typically fail, often spectacularly, driving the victim deeper into the abuser's arms while providing material to be used against you.

What does work is internal recognition. A shift that happens inside the victim when accumulated experiences create cracks in the reality the abuser has constructed. This recognition cannot be forced from outside. It emerges when the gap between what he is told and what he experiences becomes too large to bridge with rationalisation.

The Accumulation of Contradictions

Coercive control depends on the victim accepting the abuser's version of reality. She tells him what things mean, how to interpret events, what is reasonable and what is excessive. As long as he accepts her framework, he remains trapped within it.

But reality keeps intruding. Her explanations don't quite fit what he observes. Her predictions about other people's motives don't match their actual behaviour. Her assurances that things will improve if he just tries harder prove false repeatedly. Each contradiction is small enough to dismiss individually, but they accumulate.

At some point, impossible to predict when, the accumulated weight becomes too much. Something happens that cannot be explained away. A pattern becomes too clear to ignore. A moment of cruelty crosses some internal line. The structure of denial that held everything together begins to crack.

This is not a linear process. Cracks form and are repaired. Clarity emerges and is obscured again. The journey from first doubt to final departure can take months or years, with setbacks that look like total regression. Once the process starts, something fundamental has shifted.

For men, the moment when these contradictions begin to accumulate often clashes with masculine identity.

He has been taught that good men persevere, solve problems, and honour commitments. Admitting something is wrong means confronting the fear of being seen as weak, incompetent, or unable to "hold his life together." This internal conflict slows recognition. It does not stop it. It simply means the cracks emerge more quietly, and often later, than families expect.

The Role of Outside Reference Points

Isolation is central to coercive control because it removes the reference points that would help the victim evaluate his situation. When the only perspective he has access to is hers, her interpretation of reality goes unchallenged.

The continued existence of people who offer a different reality, without attacking hers directly, provides something essential. When you remain present, warm, and accepting, you become a reference point. Your stability contrasts with the chaos of his primary relationship. Your unconditional acceptance contrasts with the conditional approval he receives from her. Your consistent message that you care about him, with no strings attached, contradicts her narrative that everyone outside the relationship is hostile or unreliable.

You cannot force him to use this reference point. By maintaining it, you ensure it exists when he is ready to look.

The Recovery of the Authentic Self

Remember the adapted self-discussed earlier. The version of your son that developed to survive within the relationship. Beneath it, the authentic self remains. It has been suppressed, not destroyed.

Recovery involves the gradual re-emergence of this authentic self. Moments when he expresses genuine preferences. Occasions when he disagrees rather than accommodates. Instances when he remembers who he used to be and feels the gap between that person and who he has become.

These moments can be cultivated, gently, by connecting with the person he was before the relationship - not by pointing out how much he has changed. Instead, by engaging with interests, memories, and aspects of identity that existed before her. When you talk about shared history, recall experiences that remind him of his authentic self, or engage with interests she may have suppressed, you help keep that self accessible.

Why External Force Fails

Given that internal recognition is what matters, why not try to force that recognition? Why not present overwhelming evidence, stage an intervention, or issue ultimatums that compel him to see what you see?

The answer lies in a psychological phenomenon called reactance. When people feel their autonomy is threatened, when they feel pressured to adopt a position, they instinctively resist, even if the position makes sense. **The harder you push, the harder they push back.** This is not stubbornness or irrationality; it is a fundamental feature of human psychology.

Coercive control already involves constant pressure to adopt someone else's position. Your son's entire relationship consists of being pushed to accept his abuser's reality. When you add additional pressure from another direction, you do not liberate him from manipulation. You simply add another source of it. His response is the same: resist, defend, push back.

Moreover, interventions provide ammunition. When you attack his partner, you confirm her narrative that his family is hostile to the relationship. When you issue ultimatums, you create exactly the choice she wants him to face: her or them. When you present evidence of her abuse, you put him in the position of defending her. And each defence strengthens his commitment to the story that everything is fine.

The intervention that feels so necessary, that seems like it should work, typically achieves the opposite of its intention.

Why You Cannot Force an Awakening

This may be the hardest section of this book to accept. You have power in many areas of your life. You are accustomed to solving problems through effort, intelligence, and determination. The idea that you cannot solve this problem. That your power here is fundamentally limited, feels wrong. Surely if you just try hard enough, find the right approach, say the right words...

You cannot force an awakening. This is not a failure of love or effort. It is a structural reality of how human minds work.

The Stages of Change

Research into how people change unwanted situations. Whether addiction, unhealthy relationships, or other harmful patterns - reveals a consistent structure. People move through stages: from not recognising there is a problem, to contemplating change, to preparing for change, to taking action, to maintaining the new situation.

The critical insight is that you cannot push someone from one stage to the next. You cannot argue someone who does not see a problem into recognising one. You cannot pressure someone who is contemplating change into taking action before they're ready. Attempts to force stage progression typically backfire, pushing the person backward rather than forward.

What you can do is create conditions that support natural movement. You can avoid actions that impede progress. You can position yourself appropriately for whatever stage he's currently in. But you cannot control the timeline or force the progression.

If your son is currently in the stage where he doesn't recognise there's a problem, presenting evidence will not advance him to the next stage. He will dismiss the evidence, rationalise it, or use it as proof that you don't understand. Only his own accumulating experience can move him forward.

The Illusion of the Perfect Argument

Many families invest enormous energy in trying to construct the argument that will finally break through. If they can just explain things clearly enough, present the evidence compellingly enough, find the angle he has not considered. Surely then he will see.

This faith in the power of the perfect argument misunderstands the nature of the problem. Your son is not trapped because he lacks information or because no one has explained things clearly. He is trapped because psychological mechanisms prevent him from processing the information he already has. Adding more information, more clearly presented, does not address the underlying barrier.

Cognitive dissonance, trauma bonding, the adapted self, masculine identity. These are not information deficits. They are psychological structures that filter information to maintain a particular interpretation. The perfect argument bounces off these structures just as effectively as an imperfect one.

This doesn't mean communication is useless. It does means that the goal of communication is not to present a case that compels agreement. **The goal is to maintain connection, demonstrate unconditional love, and keep the door open.** The goal is not to win a debate.

The Trap of Trying Harder

When initial efforts fail, the natural response is to try harder. More conversations. More evidence. More emotional intensity. Surely more effort will produce results where less effort failed.

In this situation, trying harder typically makes things worse. Increased pressure increases reactance. More frequent interventions exhaust your resources while pushing him further away. The escalating emotional intensity of your efforts confirms the narrative that his family is becoming unhinged over his perfectly normal relationship.

This is counterintuitive. In most areas of life, persistence pays off. Here, persistence of the wrong kind damages the very connection you need to maintain. The answer is not to try harder. It is to try differently. And "differently" often means doing less while being more strategic about what you do.

Accepting Uncertainty

The hardest part of accepting your limited power is accepting the uncertainty that comes with it. You cannot control whether he will ever leave. You cannot guarantee a timeline. You cannot know if what you are doing is working because the effects may not be visible for months or years.

This uncertainty is genuinely painful. The desire to do something, anything that produces visible results, is overwhelming. The temptation to force the issue, to at least know where things stand, is constant.

Learning to tolerate this uncertainty without either giving up or escalating into counterproductive action is perhaps the core skill this situation requires. You are not passive; you are actively maintaining something in the face of tremendous pressure to either abandon it or destroy it through overly aggressive intervention. That is its own form of strength.

The Compassion Trap

"But she had a terrible childhood."

"She's been through so much trauma herself."

"I don't think she means to hurt him. She's just damaged."

The compassion trap catches many families. You can see that his partner has her own wounds. Her behaviour may clearly stem from her own experiences of abuse, abandonment, or neglect. She is not a monster. She is a damaged person causing damage. And knowing this makes it harder to hold her accountable.

Understanding Does Not Require Acceptance

Her history may explain her behaviour. It does not excuse it.

This distinction matters. Many people with traumatic backgrounds do not become abusive. Many manage their wounds in ways that don't harm their partners. Having been hurt does not confer the right to hurt others.

You can hold compassion for what she has been through while simultaneously holding clarity about what she is doing. These are not contradictory positions. In fact, the ability to hold both is a mark of mature moral thinking.

Her healing is not your son's responsibility to provide. If she needs help processing her trauma, that help should come from professionals, not from a partner she controls and diminishes.

The "She's Also a Victim" Paralysis

Sometimes families become so focused on understanding her pain *that they lose sight of his.*

The narrative shifts: she's the one who really needs help; he just needs to be patient; if everyone understood her better, things would improve. This narrative serves her purposes. It positions her as the wounded party deserving sympathy. It frames his suffering as secondary to hers. It suggests that the solution lies in accommodating her rather than protecting him.

Your son is the victim in your immediate concern. Whatever she has been through, he is being harmed now. Your job is not to rescue her from her history but to remain available to him in his present.

Holding Complexity Without Losing Clarity

The world contains people who are both wounded and wounding. Acknowledging her wounds does not require denying his. You can feel genuine sadness for whatever created her patterns while feeling genuine urgency about what those patterns are doing to your son.

What you cannot do is let compassion for her suffering become a reason to minimise his, excuse her behaviour, or delay your concern.

Stand Again
Support for male victims
of family violence

If anything, her visible damage should increase your concern for him. Someone who is acting out unprocessed trauma in their intimate relationship is unlikely to stop without significant intervention. Intervention that usually requires leaving the relationship or at minimum establishing boundaries she is unlikely to accept.

Compassion for her is fine. *Just don't let it cost him.*

What You CAN Do: Active Patience

If forcing change fails and passive acceptance means abandoning him, what is the middle path? The answer is active patience. A stance that is neither passive nor aggressive, that maintains presence and connection while respecting the reality of his current position.

The Distinction from Passive Acceptance

Active patience is not giving up. It is not accepting the situation as permanent. It is not abandoning hope or withdrawing your love. It is certainly not approving of what his partner is doing to him.

Passive acceptance would mean disengaging. Stepping back and waiting for something to happen. Active patience means remaining engaged, present, and strategic while recognising that direct intervention is counterproductive.

The "active" is essential. You are doing something. You are maintaining a presence that matters, providing a reference point for reality, keeping a door open that would otherwise close, and positioning yourself to be maximally useful when his internal process reaches a point where he's ready for help.

The Distinction from Enabling

Some people will suggest that maintaining connection with someone in an abusive relationship is "enabling" the abuse. This misunderstands both the dynamics of coercive control and the meaning of enabling.

Enabling means actively supporting the problematic behaviour. Making it easier for someone to continue harmful patterns without facing natural consequences. You are not enabling his partner's abuse by remaining in

contact with your son. You are not supporting the relationship by failing to attack it at every opportunity.

What you are doing is maintaining access to the person you love so that you can be there when he needs you. Cutting off contact or making the relationship conditional on his leaving would not create consequences for the abuser. It would create consequences for him, isolating him further and removing a potential lifeline.

You can maintain connection without endorsing the relationship. You can be present without being silent. You can love him unconditionally while making clear, when appropriate, that you're concerned about him.

What Active Patience Looks Like

In practice, active patience involves several components:

- **Consistent presence without pressure.** You remain in contact: calling, visiting when possible, maintaining the relationship through whatever channels remain open. Your contact is warm. It is not interrogative. You're not checking in to gather evidence or to push for action. You're checking in because you love him and want to maintain connection.

- **Unconditional acceptance of him, not the situation.** He needs to know that your love for him is not contingent on his leaving or on his agreeing with your assessment of his relationship. This doesn't mean you approve of what's happening. It means you separate your feelings about him from your feelings about his circumstances.

- **Building rapport and trust.** Every interaction that doesn't involve pressure or criticism is an investment. When you share pleasant experiences, talk about neutral topics, and demonstrate that time with you is enjoyable rather than fraught, you build the relational capital you will need when he's ready to turn to someone for help.

- **Planting seeds without forcing growth.** Occasionally, gently, you can introduce perspectives or ask questions that invite reflection without demanding change. These are not arguments or interventions. They are seeds planted in soil you cannot control. Some may take root; many will not. The planting matters; the outcome is not in your hands.

- **Maintaining your own life and wellbeing.** Active patience is sustainable only if you are sustaining yourself. This is not selfish; it is strategic. You are in this for the long term, potentially years. Burning out in six months helps no one. Taking care of yourself is part of the strategy.

The Posture You Need

Beyond specific actions, active patience requires a particular internal posture. A way of being in relation to your son and his situation that shapes how you show up in every interaction.

Warmth Over Confrontation

Research into what helps people change unwanted patterns consistently finds that warmth and empathy outperform confrontation. This applies to addiction, to relationship difficulties, to any situation where someone needs to recognise a problem and take action to address it.

Confrontation feels satisfying because it expresses the urgency you feel. But warmth is what creates openings. A person who feels judged becomes defensive. A person who feels accepted becomes open. Your son is already surrounded by judgment and conditional acceptance in his primary relationship. Offering something different: genuine warmth without strings, is more powerful than you might expect.

This does not mean you can never express concern or disagreement. It means that warmth is the foundation, not an occasional addition. He should experience contact with you as a relief from the stress of his primary relationship. Not as another source of pressure.

Curiosity Over Assumption

You think you know what is happening in his relationship, and you may be largely correct. Approaching him with assumptions, even accurate ones, puts him in a defensive position. He must either agree with your assessment, which triggers all the barriers to recognition discussed earlier, or defend against it.

Curiosity creates a different dynamic. When you ask genuine questions about his life and listen to the answers, you learn more about his actual experience. You may discover things you didn't know. You demonstrate respect for his perspective even when you suspect that perspective has been distorted.

Questions also invite him to articulate his situation in his own words, which can surface contradictions that your assertions would not. "How are things going?" followed by genuine listening may do more than any argument you could construct.

Patience Over Urgency

Every instinct tells you that this is urgent. He is suffering now. The relationship is causing damage now. Waiting feels like complicity in ongoing harm.

Urgency communicated becomes pressure, and pressure triggers resistance. The timeline of his readiness is not something you can accelerate through the intensity of your concern. Paradoxically, conveying calm patience, even when you do not feel it, may create more space for movement than conveying the urgency you genuinely feel.

This is not the same as saying nothing is urgent. Safety concerns are legitimately urgent and require different responses. The general project of helping him recognise his situation and eventually leave is a long-term endeavour, and treating it as an emergency typically undermines it.

Steadiness Over Reactivity

His situation will trigger strong emotions in you: fear, anger, frustration, grief. These emotions are legitimate and need somewhere to go. They should not go directly into your interactions with him.

Steadiness is a gift you can offer. His primary relationship is characterised by unpredictability and emotional volatility. You can be the opposite. A consistent, calm presence that does not fluctuate based on the latest development or your current emotional state.

This requires finding other outlets for your emotional responses. Therapy for yourself, support from friends who understand the situation, perhaps a support group for families of abuse victims. Your feelings matter and need processing. He should not be the one processing them with you.

The Long View

Adopting these postures requires constantly reminding yourself of the long view. Each individual interaction may feel inconsequential or frustrating. The conversation you had last week did not produce any visible change. The visit where you bit your tongue and said nothing about the relationship seemed like a waste.

You are not building toward a single moment of breakthrough. You are maintaining a relationship that will matter whenever he's ready. Every warm interaction deposits something in the account you will draw upon later. Every demonstration of unconditional love reminds him that he is valued for who he is, not just for what he provides.

Professional support workers leave after the intervention ends. Therapists are available only during scheduled sessions. You are the one who remains. Through months, through years, through setbacks and false starts. Your steady presence is not a failure to act dramatically. It is the most powerful thing you can offer.

KEY TAKEAWAYS:

- **CHANGE COMES FROM INSIDE, NOT OUTSIDE.**

- **YOU CANNOT FORCE YOUR SON'S AWAKENING, BUT YOU CAN CREATE CONDITIONS THAT SUPPORT IT:**

- **BY MAINTAINING WARM CONNECTION WITHOUT PRESSURE, BY BEING A STABLE REFERENCE POINT FOR REALITY, AND BY POSITIONING YOURSELF TO BE THERE WHEN HE'S READY.**

- **THIS IS ACTIVE PATIENCE. NEITHER PASSIVE ACCEPTANCE NOR COUNTERPRODUCTIVE INTERVENTION, BUT STRATEGIC PRESENCE SUSTAINED ACROSS TIME.**

Chapter 4: Leaving the Light On

Active patience needs a concrete framework. This chapter explains what it means to 'leave the light on' for someone trapped in coercive control, and establishes the principles that will guide your approach.

What "Leaving the Light On" Actually Means

The metaphor of leaving a light on captures something essential about what you're doing. When someone is lost in darkness, you cannot go in and drag them out. But you can ensure there's a visible beacon guiding them home when they're ready to move.

Your son is, in a very real sense, lost. The relationship has taken him somewhere he would not have chosen to go, somewhere he cannot clearly see. The path back is obscured by psychological barriers, practical complications, and the abuser's active efforts to keep him isolated.

Leaving the light on means maintaining something he can orient toward A relationship that remains intact, love that remains unconditional, a door that remains open no matter how long he takes to walk through it.

The Light Is the Relationship

The light is not a message or an argument. It is the relationship itself. Your continued presence in his life, your demonstrated care, your refusal to abandon him regardless of his choices.

This relationship provides several things he needs:

- **A connection outside her control.** His partner works to isolate him because outside relationships threaten her influence. Every relationship he maintains is a thread connecting him to a larger world beyond the one she has constructed.

- **A different model of relationship.** His primary experience of intimacy has become warped. Your unconditional love provides a contrast: a reminder that relationships can exist without constant performance, that acceptance can be given freely rather than earned through compliance.

- **A safety net for when he's ready.** Leaving an abusive relationship is terrifying. Knowing that someone will be there, that he won't be alone, makes the prospect less overwhelming. Your maintained relationship is his insurance policy.

- **A reminder of who he was.** You knew him before. You carry memories of the person he was prior to this relationship. Your continued presence connects him to that earlier self, which remains inside him even when it seems inaccessible.

What the Light Is Not

Leaving the light on does not mean:

- **Constant pressure to leave.** A light doesn't chase. It simply remains visible. If every interaction involves pushing him to leave, you become another source of pressure rather than a refuge from it. The light that follows him around demanding he come home is not a beacon; it's a searchlight.

- **Pretending everything is fine.** You don't need to endorse the relationship or act as though you have no concerns. Leaving the light on is compatible with having expressed, once and clearly, that you're worried about him. It simply means not making that worry the content of every interaction.

- **Accepting poor treatment.** If he is treating you badly: cancelling plans, speaking disrespectfully, allowing his partner to attack you, you can maintain boundaries while keeping the light on. The light represents your love and availability, not your willingness to absorb abuse yourself.

- **Waiting passively.** As discussed in the previous chapter, this is active, not passive. You are maintaining the light, which requires effort and intentionality. You are not simply sitting and hoping something changes.

Men can sometimes retreat further when they sense they are disappointing the people they love. Keeping the light on without criticism allows him to approach you when he feels safe enough to risk being seen.

The Light Must Survive the Storm

For this metaphor to work, the light must remain on through whatever comes. There will be periods of no contact. There will be hurtful words. There will be times when he seems to have completely rejected you in favour of her version of reality.

The light must survive all of this. Your commitment to remaining present for him cannot be contingent on his current behaviour or on whether he seems to be responding. The whole point is that you are there regardless. That your love is not conditional on his making progress on your timeline.

This is demanding. It requires managing your own hurt and frustration rather than letting them extinguish your availability. It requires remembering that his current self is not his authentic self, and that the rejection you're experiencing comes from the adapted self that developed to survive his relationship.

But it is essential. A light that flickers out when conditions become difficult is not a reliable beacon. He needs to know (to trust at a level deeper than conscious thought) that you will be there whenever he's ready, however long that takes, whatever happens in between.

The Principles

The specific situations you'll encounter are impossible to predict, so rigid rules are less useful than principles you can apply across circumstances. These principles should guide your decisions about how to interact with your son and respond to the challenges that arise.

Core Principles for Leaving the Light On

Principle	What It Means in Practice
Connection First	Every interaction should prioritise maintaining the relationship. Before saying or doing anything, ask: will this strengthen or weaken our connection? If it might damage the relationship, it should be reconsidered.
No Ultimatums	Never force a choice between you and her. Ultimatums feel powerful but consistently backfire. He may not choose you, and then both of you are stuck with consequences neither wanted. Keep the door open unconditionally.
Respond to Him, Not Her	Your relationship is with your son. While you cannot ignore his partner's existence, your focus should be on him, on his wellbeing, his experience, his needs. Attacks on her become attacks on him, since he currently identifies with the relationship.
Actions Over Arguments	Demonstrate your love through consistent presence and unconditional support rather than trying to convince him through words. Arguments can be debated; actions accumulate as evidence of who you are and what you offer.
Questions Over Statements	When you do engage with his situation, questions invite reflection more effectively than statements. "How did that make you feel?" opens something that "She shouldn't treat you that way" closes. Let him arrive at conclusions rather than presenting them.

Principle	What It Means in Practice
His Timeline, Not Yours	You cannot control when he's ready to see clearly or take action. Accept that his internal process has its own pace. Rushing creates resistance; patience creates space for natural movement.
Protect Yourself Too	You cannot sustain this indefinitely if you're being destroyed in the process. Boundaries that protect your wellbeing are legitimate and necessary. The light must survive the storm and that requires fuel.

Applying the Principles

These principles sometimes tension with each other. Connection first might suggest avoiding any difficult topics, but protecting yourself might require setting a boundary. His timeline, not yours, might suggest infinite patience, but no ultimatums doesn't mean accepting any treatment indefinitely.

There is no formula that resolves these tensions in advance. You will need to apply judgment in specific situations, guided by these principles but not mechanically following any single one. The goal is not perfection but continuous effort in the right direction, with repair when you misstep.

The later chapters of this book will apply these principles to specific stages and situations. For now, absorb them as the foundation of your approach. When you're unsure what to do, return to these principles and ask which response best honours them given the specific circumstances you face.

The Cumulative Power of Small Things

This approach can feel underwhelming. You want to do something significant, something that matters, something that produces visible results. Staying warm and present, asking gentle questions, maintaining connection without pressure, it doesn't feel like enough.

But small things accumulate. Every warm interaction deposits something. Every demonstration of unconditional love adds to the evidence that contradicts his partner's narrative. Every moment of calm connection reminds him of what exists outside the chaos of his primary relationship.

You are not building toward a single transformative moment. You are maintaining something that matters, interaction by interaction, week by week, month by month. This sustained presence is not dramatic, but it is powerful. Professional intervention lasts hours; you last years. The relationship you maintain will still be there when all the interventions have faded.

Trust the process, even when you cannot see results. Your love, expressed through consistent presence and unconditional acceptance, is doing more than you know.

KEY TAKEAWAYS:

- **"LEAVING THE LIGHT ON" MEANS MAINTAINING YOUR RELATIONSHIP AS A VISIBLE BEACON HE CAN ORIENT TOWARD WHEN HE'S READY.**

- **THIS REQUIRES CONSISTENT PRESENCE WITHOUT PRESSURE, GUIDED BY PRINCIPLES THAT PRIORITISE CONNECTION, AVOID ULTIMATUMS, AND RESPECT HIS TIMELINE WHILE PROTECTING YOUR OWN WELLBEING.**

- **THE CUMULATIVE POWER OF SUSTAINED WARMTH AND UNCONDITIONAL LOVE SHOULD NOT BE UNDERESTIMATED.**

PART THREE: BUILDING A UNIFIED FAMILY FRONT

Chapter 5: Working Together

You are probably not the only person who loves him. Parents, siblings, extended family, close friends - others are watching this unfold and feeling their own urgency to help. How these people coordinate their efforts matters enormously. A unified approach amplifies your collective presence; an uncoordinated one creates chaos that his partner can exploit.

Getting Family Aligned

The first step toward effective support is ensuring that everyone who cares about your son understands what they're dealing with and agrees on how to approach it. This is harder than it sounds. Different family members have different relationships with him, different emotional responses to the situation, and different instincts about what should be done.

Shared Understanding

Before you can coordinate action, you need shared understanding. This means everyone involved grasping the nature of coercive control, the reasons why direct intervention typically fails, and the principles of leaving the light on.

This book can serve as a starting point. Ask key family members to read it, or at minimum to read Parts One and Two. You can also point them to the Stand Again Blueprint of Family Violence Against Men and the TTI model (Tactic → Trigger → Impact). These give everyone a shared language for what you are seeing, so you are not arguing about vague impressions but working from the same map.

The concepts are counterintuitive, and people who haven't absorbed them will default to their natural instincts: which often mean well-intentioned actions that make things worse.

Expect resistance. Some family members will feel that the approach outlined here is too passive, that waiting is complicity, that something more dramatic needs to happen. These objections need to be heard and discussed. The person who goes rogue and attempts their own intervention can undo months of careful positioning by the rest of the family.

What matters is arriving at genuine agreement, not just compliance. A family member who superficially agrees but actually believes you're all being too passive will eventually act on their real beliefs. Better to have the argument now, thoroughly, than to discover the disagreement when someone has already done damage.

Assigning Roles

Different family members occupy different positions in your son's life, and these differences can be leveraged strategically.

Consider who has the best current access. Whose calls does he still answer? Who can visit without triggering his partner's defensive responses? This person should be protected as a communication channel. They should not be the one to raise difficult topics or push boundaries, because doing so might close the channel.

Consider who has emotional credibility. Sometimes a sibling can say things a parent cannot. Sometimes an uncle or family friend occupies a position of respect that creates different openings. Think about who he might actually listen to if he were ever ready to hear something difficult.

Consider who can handle specific practical roles. Who will be the person he calls at 3am if he finally decides to leave? Who has the resources to offer emergency housing? Who has legal or financial expertise that might be needed? Knowing who does what prevents scrambling when the moment arrives.

None of this requires formal assignment, but the conversation should happen. When the family understands who is positioned for what, coordination becomes possible.

Managing Family Disagreements

Families are not monoliths. You will have disagreements about what to do, how serious the situation is, and who is to blame. These disagreements are normal but can become destructive if they fragment the family's response.

Some common fault lines:

- **"You're overreacting" versus "You're not doing enough."** Some family members may not see the situation as seriously as you do. They may have less information, less contact, or simply a different threshold for concern. Conversely, some may think you're being too passive. These perspectives need to be reconciled through honest conversation about what everyone is observing.

- **Blame directed at him.** Some family members may hold your son responsible for his situation. "He chose this." "He just has to man up." "A real man would know better." This response often comes from people who don't understand how coercive control works. Education about the psychological mechanisms involved can help shift this perspective.

- **Blame directed at you.** Parents sometimes receive blame from extended family: "How did you raise him to accept this?" "You should have seen this coming." This is painful and unproductive. Part One of this book addresses why coercive control is not a failure of upbringing.

- **Different relationships with his partner.** Some family members may actually like his partner or have been successfully charmed by her public persona. They may struggle to believe the person they've experienced could be doing what you're describing. Remember that the difference between her public and private face is part of the dynamic.

When these disagreements arise, try to focus on observable facts rather than interpretations. What have people actually witnessed? What has he actually said? Building from shared observations is more productive than arguing about conclusions.

Practical Communication

Once the family is aligned, practical communication becomes essential. You need ways to share information, coordinate responses, and support each other through what will be a demanding process.

Information Sharing

Different family members will observe different things. Someone might notice he's lost weight during a video call. Someone else might receive a text message that seems off. A third person might hear through mutual friends that things are tense. No single person has the complete picture.

Create a way to share these observations without requiring formal meetings. A group text thread, a shared document, or regular phone calls can serve this purpose. The goal is to maintain collective awareness of his situation so that changes (positive or concerning) are noticed.

Be thoughtful about security. If his partner has access to his phone or accounts, messages sent to him may be monitored. The family communication channel should be separate from any communication that might reach her.

Consistent Messaging

When multiple people are in contact with your son, the messages he receives should be consistent. This doesn't mean everyone says the same scripted words, but the underlying themes should align.

The core message should be: we love you unconditionally, we're here for you no matter what, and our door is always open. Variations are fine; contradictions are not. If Dad is communicating acceptance while his sister is issuing ultimatums, the mixed signals create confusion and provide material for his partner to exploit.

Discuss in advance how to handle specific topics. What will you say if he asks directly whether you like his partner? What will you say if he announces an engagement or pregnancy? Having thought through these scenarios together helps ensure consistent responses.

Coordinating Contact

If contact with him is limited, coordinating who reaches out and when prevents overwhelming him with attention that might trigger his partner's suspicion or his own defensiveness.

Consider staggering contact so that he hears from different family members at different times, rather than receiving a wave of calls or messages that feels like an organised campaign. Organic contact is less likely to raise alarm bells than contact that appears coordinated.

If someone has an important conversation or learns something significant, let others know before they reach out. This prevents the situation where three different family members ask about the same thing, making the concern feel like an interrogation.

Messages That Work and Messages That Backfire

The specific words you use matter. Some messages open doors; others close them. Understanding the difference helps everyone in the family communicate more effectively.

Comparing Message Approaches

Messages That Open Doors	Messages That Close Doors
"I love you and I'm always here for you."	"I love you, but I can't watch you destroy yourself."
"How are you doing? I've been thinking about you."	"Is she treating you badly again? What's going on?"
"Remember when we used to [shared positive memory]?"	"You've changed so much since you met her."
"If you ever need anything, I'm here. No questions asked."	"When are you going to leave? You know you need to."

Messages That Open Doors	Messages That Close Doors
"That sounds really hard. How are you coping?"	"She's abusing you. Why can't you see that?"
"I miss spending time with you."	"She's isolated you from everyone who cares about you."

Notice the pattern. Messages that open doors focus on him, on your relationship with him, and on unconditional support. Messages that close doors focus on her, on his failures, and on conditions for your continued relationship.

The door-opening messages are not passive or weak. "I'm always here for you" is a statement of commitment. "If you ever need anything, no questions asked" signals readiness to help when he's ready. These messages do work. They maintain connection and position you for when he needs you.

The door-closing messages feel more direct and powerful, which is why they're tempting. But they trigger defence, confirm his partner's narrative about family hostility, and close precisely the doors you need to keep open.

What Not to Do

Beyond ineffective messaging, certain approaches are actively harmful. Ensuring the entire family understands these pitfalls helps prevent well-intentioned actions that cause damage.

The Formal Intervention

Gathering family and friends to confront the person with a unified message demanding change has a place in addiction treatment, though even there its effectiveness is debated. In coercive control situations, it is almost always counterproductive.

An intervention puts your son in a position where he must choose sides in front of an audience. He is likely to choose the relationship, both because of the psychological mechanisms keeping him there and because public confrontation activates pride and defensiveness. He will leave the intervention more committed to his partner, more alienated from you, and with evidence that she was right about his family being against them.

His partner will learn about the intervention. He will tell her, or she will find out. This provides her with ammunition: proof that his family is hostile, that they're trying to separate you, that they cannot be trusted. Everything she has said about you will feel confirmed.

The aftermath may include total estrangement. Doors that were partially open will slam shut. Access you had will be revoked. The intervention that was supposed to solve everything will have made everything worse.

Attacking His Partner Directly

The urge to confront the person hurting your son is powerful. You want to tell her what you think of her, demand she change her behaviour, or warn her about consequences. This feels like protecting him.

Direct confrontation with an abuser typically escalates the situation. She may increase control over him, restrict his contact with you, or punish him for his family's behaviour. You cannot control her; you can only give her reasons to tighten her grip.

Additionally, your attack on her becomes an attack on him in his current psychology. He identifies with the relationship. When you attack her, he experiences it as an attack on his choices, his judgment, his life. He will defend her and each defence strengthens his commitment to the story that she is misunderstood and you are the problem.

Ultimatums and Conditions

"If you don't leave her, I'm done." "I won't speak to you as long as you're with her." "It's us or her."

These ultimatums feel like drawing a necessary line. They express the depth of your concern and the seriousness of the situation. But they create exactly the dynamic his partner wants: a forced choice between her and his family.

If he chooses her (which is likely given where he is psychologically) you have now lost access entirely. You cannot leave the light on from a position of

estrangement. Your absence from his life removes a reference point he needs, and your conditional love confirms her narrative that outside relationships are unsafe.

If he does leave under the pressure of an ultimatum, the decision is not his. He has not done the internal work necessary for sustainable separation. The likelihood of returning to her is high, and your relationship will be damaged by the coercion, even if it "worked."

Gathering Evidence to Convince Him

Families sometimes invest enormous energy in building a case: documenting her behaviour, collecting testimony from others who have witnessed problems, researching coercive control so they can present it like a legal brief. Surely if the evidence is overwhelming enough, he will have to accept the truth.

This misunderstands the problem. He is not failing to see the evidence; he is interpreting the evidence through a framework that explains it away. More evidence processed through the same framework produces the same result. The breakthrough you're hoping for will not come from a sufficiently compelling presentation of facts.

Moreover, presenting your evidence places him in a defensive position. He must argue against your case, which strengthens his commitment to his position. Each rebuttal he offers, each explanation for why you've misunderstood, deepens his investment in the alternative story.

Going Behind His Back

Contacting his employer, his friends, or others in his life to express your concerns without his knowledge is tempting when you feel powerless. Perhaps if other people raise issues, he'll listen to them.

This approach typically backfires. When he discovers what you've done (and he likely will) he will feel betrayed. His partner will use this as evidence that you cannot be trusted, that you operate behind his back, that you're trying to manipulate his life. Trust that took years to build can be destroyed in a single well-intentioned call.

Your relationship with him is your channel of influence. Protecting that relationship means not doing things that would damage it if discovered.

Flying Monkeys in Your Network

A "flying monkey" is someone who, often unknowingly, does an abuser's work for her. The term comes from the flying monkeys in The Wizard of Oz who do the witch's bidding. In coercive control dynamics, flying monkeys spread the abuser's version of reality, apply pressure on her behalf, and gather information that flows back to her.

You may have flying monkeys in your own network without realising it. These might be:

- **Family members who have been charmed.** His partner may have successfully won over certain relatives. These people may report back to her about family discussions, defend her to others, or pressure your son to be more understanding of her needs.

- **Mutual friends who don't see the full picture.** Friends who only see her public persona may carry messages, apply social pressure, or tell your son his family is overreacting.

- **People who believe they're helping.** Sometimes well-meaning people conclude that the way to help is to encourage reconciliation, smooth things over, or pressure both sides to get along. They become unwitting agents of the status quo.

Be thoughtful about what you share and with whom. Information about your concerns or your strategy may make its way back to his partner through channels you didn't anticipate. This isn't about paranoia; it's about recognising that in a coercive control dynamic, information is power, and she is actively gathering it.

When you identify someone who seems to be operating as a flying monkey, you have choices.

- You can **limit what you share** with them.

- You can **factor their presence into your planning**, ensuring that sensitive information and strategy discussions don't include them.

- You can gently attempt to **open their eyes** to what's happening. However use your judgement here as your attempts may be communicated to the abuser.

Remember that many people still do not recognise male victims at all. A relative or friend who insists he cannot be abused because he is a man is unlikely to be a safe ally and may slide into the role of carrying the abuser's narrative without realising it.

KEY TAKEAWAYS:

- **A COORDINATED FAMILY APPROACH IS MORE POWERFUL THAN FRAGMENTED INDIVIDUAL EFFORTS.**

- **THIS REQUIRES SHARED UNDERSTANDING OF WHAT YOU'RE DEALING WITH, AGREEMENT ON PRINCIPLES, CONSISTENT MESSAGING, AND CLEAR COMMUNICATION CHANNELS.**

- **EQUALLY IMPORTANT IS UNDERSTANDING WHAT NOT TO DO: FORMAL INTERVENTIONS, ULTIMATUMS, AND DIRECT ATTACKS ON HIS PARTNER TYPICALLY MAKE THINGS WORSE.**

- **BE AWARE THAT SOME PEOPLE IN YOUR NETWORK MAY, KNOWINGLY OR UNKNOWINGLY, BE WORKING AGAINST YOUR EFFORTS.**

Chapter 6: Sustaining Yourself

This may be a long journey. Months, possibly years. You cannot sustain the effort required if you are not taking care of yourself. This chapter addresses the emotional toll families experience, how to build support, and how to maintain hope without being destroyed by it.

The Emotional Toll on Families

What you are experiencing is a form of grief. But it's complicated grief, because the person you're mourning is still alive. Your son exists, you may even see him occasionally, but the relationship you had and the person you knew seem to have disappeared. This ambiguous loss is particularly difficult to process.

The Grief That Has No Name

When someone dies, the grief is acknowledged. Rituals exist. People offer condolences. Time off work is expected. The pain is legitimised by social recognition.

Your loss has no such recognition. Your son is alive, so what are you grieving? The relationship appears intact. You may still exchange occasional texts or see each other at holidays, so how can you claim to have lost him? Friends who haven't experienced this may minimise your pain or suggest you're overreacting.

But you have lost something real. You've lost easy access to your child. You've lost the relationship you had. You've lost the future you imagined, the grandchildren you'd see regularly, the holidays that felt natural, the phone calls that didn't feel monitored or guarded. These losses are real and deserve acknowledgment, even if the person at the centre of them is technically still present.

Secondary Trauma

Watching someone you love be harmed creates its own trauma. You may experience symptoms similar to those of abuse victims: hypervigilance, intrusive thoughts, difficulty sleeping, anxiety when the phone rings, and emotional numbness alternating with overwhelming feeling.

This is not weakness or overreaction. It is a normal response to an abnormal situation. Your nervous system is reacting to sustained threat. Not threat to yourself, but threat to someone you love, which your brain processes similarly.

Taking your own psychological responses seriously is essential. If you are experiencing significant distress, professional support is not an indulgence but a practical necessity. You cannot leave the light on if you have burned yourself out.

The Hijacking of Your Life

One insidious effect of this situation is how it can consume your entire existence. Every thought returns to him. Every piece of news gets evaluated through the lens of what it might mean for his situation. Your own life (your work, your other relationships, your interests) gets pushed aside as you become consumed by the crisis.

This is understandable but not sustainable. If your entire identity becomes "person trying to save their son," you lose the foundation you need to remain stable and present. Your other relationships suffer. Your health suffers. You become less capable, not more, of helping when the time comes.

Reclaiming your own life is not abandoning him. It is ensuring you have something left to offer when he needs you.

Building Your Support System

You need people who understand what you're going through and can provide the support you need to continue. Building this support deliberately is essential.

Professional Help

A therapist or coach (such as Stand Again) who understands coercive control dynamics can be invaluable. They provide a space to process your emotions without burdening your son or other family members. They can help you maintain perspective, develop coping strategies, and work through the complicated feelings that arise.

Look for someone with experience in domestic abuse, family systems, or trauma. General therapists may not fully understand the dynamics at play. Some therapists, unfortunately, may suggest approaches that sound reasonable in normal relationship difficulties but are counterproductive in coercive control situations: like encouraging direct communication or family therapy that would include the abuser.

If you find a therapist who doesn't seem to understand, it's appropriate to find someone else. Not all professionals have training in this area, and working with someone who doesn't understand can be frustrating rather than helpful.

Support Groups

Connecting with others in similar situations provides something that even the best therapist cannot: the understanding of people who truly know what you're experiencing. Online groups for parents of adults in abusive relationships exist and can offer community, practical advice, and the comfort of being believed.

Where possible, look for spaces that recognise male victims explicitly. General domestic violence forums can still be helpful, although some carry assumptions about men that will not fit your reality. A mix of general support and male-focused resources - such as Stand Again content or other father-focused communities - often gives a more accurate mirror of what you are living through.

These groups also provide reality checks. When you wonder if you're overreacting, seeing others with identical experiences validates your perceptions. When you feel alone, discovering hundreds of people in the

same situation reminds you that this is a recognised phenomenon, not something you've imagined.

Be somewhat cautious about advice in online groups. Not all advice is good advice, and some people may recommend approaches this book counsels against. Filter suggestions through the principles you've learned, and don't let the urgency of others push you toward counterproductive action.

Trusted Friends

One or two trusted friends who understand the situation and can listen without judgment are essential. These are people you can call when you need to vent, when you've received upsetting news, or when you just need to be reminded that you're not crazy.

Choose carefully. Some people will not understand, and explaining the situation to people who respond with unhelpful advice or minimisation is exhausting. The right person is someone who can listen, validate your experience, and support you without needing you to constantly justify your concern.

Be mindful of how much you lean on any single person. Even the most supportive friend can experience compassion fatigue. Distributing your support needs across multiple sources: professional help, support groups, friends, family, prevents overwhelming any one person.

Managing Hope

Hope is necessary for continuing. Without hope that things can improve, the effort of maintaining your presence becomes unbearable. But hope can also be destructive if it creates expectations that set you up for repeated devastation.

The Problem with Attached Hope

Attached hope is hope tied to specific outcomes or timelines. "He'll realise by Christmas." "Once she does X, he'll finally see." "This is the year he'll leave." When these expectations aren't met, and they usually aren't met, the disappointment is crushing.

The pattern of raised and dashed hope is exhausting. Each cycle takes something out of you. After enough cycles, you may find yourself emotionally depleted, bitter, or tempted to give up entirely.

Sustainable Hope

Sustainable hope is hope without attachment to specific outcomes or timelines. It is hope that holds open the possibility that things can improve, without expecting improvement on any particular schedule.

This kind of hope says: "I believe he can eventually see clearly and find his way home. I don't know when that will be or what it will take. I am committing to being here regardless, and I am not attaching my wellbeing to whether it happens this month or this year."

Sustainable hope coexists with uncertainty. It doesn't require knowing how the story ends. It allows you to continue the work of maintaining connection without the emotional volatility of constantly rising and falling expectations.

Practicing Detachment from Outcomes

Detachment from outcomes doesn't mean not caring. It means caring about the person while releasing your grip on how things unfold. You do what you can do: maintain connection, leave the light on, take care of yourself and you let go of what you cannot control, which is everything else.

This is easier to describe than to do. Every parent reading this will feel the impossibility of truly releasing attachment to their child's wellbeing. Complete detachment isn't the goal; working toward a healthier relationship with outcomes is.

Mindfulness practices, therapy, support groups, and spiritual traditions all offer approaches to cultivating this kind of detachment. Find what works for you. The goal is to be able to continue, to maintain hope and effort, without being destroyed by outcomes you cannot control.

Maintaining Your Other Relationships

The crisis with your son can eclipse everything else in your life. But you have other relationships that matter and that need attention: your partner, your other children, your friends, your extended family. These relationships are not distractions from the important thing; they are part of what sustains you to continue.

Your Partner

If you have a spouse or partner, they are likely experiencing their own version of this grief and stress. Or they may be experiencing it differently in ways that create friction. Couples sometimes find themselves divided by this crisis: disagreeing about what to do, blaming each other for the situation, or simply being too consumed by their own pain to support each other.

Protect this relationship. You need each other. Make time to connect about things other than your son. Check in about how each of you is coping. If significant tension is developing, couples counselling can help you navigate this crisis together rather than letting it drive you apart.

Remember that your partner may be at a different place in processing this situation. One of you may have accepted the need for active patience while the other is still pushing for more direct intervention. Work toward alignment, but with compassion for how hard this is for both of you.

Your Other Children

If you have other children, they are watching how you handle this. They may be experiencing their own grief about their sibling. And they may be wondering, consciously or not, whether your love for them is as unconditional as you say your love for their brother is.

Be careful not to let the crisis with one child consume the attention that your other children need. They deserve parents who are present for their lives, not parents who are so absorbed in their sibling's drama that everything else becomes secondary.

Their developmental needs don't pause because you're in crisis. They need you now, in the ways that children need parents, and that need is legitimate.

This is especially true if you have sons who are watching how you respond. They are learning, quietly, what happens to a man in your family when he struggles, and whether there is room for male pain without rejection or ridicule.

Your Friends and Your Self

Friendships outside the family provide perspective and relief. Maintaining these connections (even when you don't feel like socialising, even when your mind is elsewhere) keeps you connected to a world beyond the crisis.

Similarly, maintaining activities that bring you joy, exercise that keeps you healthy, and practices that sustain your spirit are not selfish indulgences. They are strategic necessities. You are running a marathon, not a sprint. Depleting yourself in the first mile helps no one.

Give yourself permission to have moments of happiness that have nothing to do with your son. This is not betrayal. Your capacity for joy is not a finite resource that, if spent elsewhere, leaves less for him. Taking care of yourself makes you more capable, not less, of being there for him when the time comes.

When Other Family Members Give Up

You may find yourself increasingly alone in this vigil. Extended family who were once concerned have moved on. Siblings have decided it is not worth the heartache. Your partner is exhausted by the topic. People who once asked how things were going have stopped asking.

This is isolating. You are carrying hope that others have set down. You are maintaining a watch that no one else seems willing to keep. And alongside your own grief and worry, you may find yourself managing theirs. The uncle who has become bitter. The grandparent who cries every time his name comes up. The sibling who has moved from concern to anger.

Some realities to hold: People have different capacities. Some people cannot sustain uncertainty for years. Their withdrawal is not betrayal. It is limitation.

They may return when circumstances change. You cannot carry everyone. If you are spending as much energy managing family members' emotions as you are maintaining connection with your son, something needs to shift.

You are allowed to set boundaries. "I understand this is hard for you. I'm not able to process your feelings about this right now." Find your core team. Even one or two people who remain committed makes a difference. Quality matters more than quantity. Identify who is actually helping and invest there.

The loneliness is real. Name it. You are doing something hard, and you are increasingly doing it alone. This deserves acknowledgment, not minimisation. Your sustained presence matters even if you are the only one.

The light does not need to be held by a crowd. One person, steady and consistent, is enough.

When You Want to Give Up

There will be moments when you cannot do this anymore. When the weight is too heavy. When hope feels like self-deception. When you look at the years stretching ahead and think: I cannot continue.

This is not weakness. This is the reasonable response of a human being to sustained unresolvable pain.

When you hit this wall: Let yourself feel it fully. The despair, the exhaustion, the grief, the rage. Do not push it away. Do not tell yourself you should be stronger. Sit in it. It will not destroy you, though it may feel like it will.

Distinguish between feeling like giving up and actually giving up. You can feel utterly hopeless and still send the birthday text. The feeling does not require action. It requires acknowledgment. Reach for support. This is the moment for your therapist, your support group, your most trusted friend.

Remember that giving up is also a choice you can make. You are not obligated to maintain this vigil forever at any cost. If you reach a point where continuing is genuinely destroying you, stepping back is an option. This is not failure. It is self-preservation.

Some parents need to create distance to survive. If you reach that point, you can leave the door unlocked without standing at it.

Most often, the moment passes. You rest. You cry. You rage. And then something in you gets up again. You send another message into the silence. You show up at another family gathering where his absence aches. You continue.

This is not because you are superhuman. It is because love is stubborn and does not follow logic. You continue because you cannot imagine not continuing. And that is enough.

KEY TAKEAWAY:

- **YOU CANNOT POUR FROM AN EMPTY CUP.**

- **THE EMOTIONAL TOLL OF THIS SITUATION IS REAL AND SERIOUS, AND SUSTAINING YOURSELF THROUGH WHAT MAY BE A LONG JOURNEY REQUIRES DELIBERATE EFFORT:**

- **PROFESSIONAL SUPPORT, CONNECTION WITH OTHERS WHO UNDERSTAND, MANAGING HOPE IN SUSTAINABLE WAYS, AND PROTECTING YOUR OTHER RELATIONSHIPS AND YOUR OWN WELLBEING.**

- **TAKING CARE OF YOURSELF IS NOT SELFISHNESS; IT IS STRATEGY.**

PART FOUR: THE JOURNEY

Understanding the Stages

The journey from deep entrapment to freedom does not happen all at once. It unfolds through recognisable stages, each with its own characteristics, challenges, and opportunities. Understanding these stages helps you calibrate your approach to where your son actually is, rather than where you wish he were.

A few important caveats before we proceed:

- **Stages are not linear.** Your son may move forward and then regress. He may show signs of one stage while still primarily operating in another. He may skip stages or seem to occupy multiple stages simultaneously. These descriptions are maps, not rails.

- **You cannot push him through stages.** Understanding the stages may create temptation to accelerate his progress. This temptation should be resisted. The principles from Part Two apply throughout: warmth over pressure, presence over intervention, his timeline not yours.

- **Your perception may be incomplete.** You see only what he shows you, and what he shows you is filtered through the adapted self. His internal reality may be different from what you observe. Hold your assessments loosely.

Each of the following chapters describes one stage: what it looks like, what he's experiencing internally, what his partner is likely doing, what he needs from you, specific scenarios you might encounter, and how to position yourself for the possibility of movement. The final stage includes additional material on the particular challenges of reconstruction.

Chapter 7: Stage One - Deep in the System

This is where most families are when they pick up this book. He is fully immersed in the reality his partner has constructed. He cannot see that anything is wrong because he is operating entirely within her framework. This stage can last months or years. It is often the most painful to witness. And the one that requires the most patience, the most restraint, and the clearest understanding of what you can and cannot do.

Recognising This Stage

Stage One is characterised by complete absorption in the relationship and complete acceptance of the abuser's framework. Your son genuinely believes everything is fine. Or if not fine, that any problems are his responsibility to fix.

Signs that he is in Stage One:

- **He defends her vigorously** if you express any concern, often with explanations that sound rehearsed or that echo her language.

- **He seems unable to acknowledge problems** in the relationship or frames all problems as his own failures.

- **He has significantly reduced contact** with friends and family and seems content with this isolation.

- **His personality seems altered**: flatter, more guarded, less spontaneous than the person you knew.

- **He checks with her before making plans**, even minor ones, and seems anxious about her reactions.

- **He prioritises her needs** and preferences so completely that his own seem to have disappeared.

- **He presents a unified front** with her, speaking in "we" rather than "I" and deferring to her interpretation of events.

From outside, this looks like a man who has been replaced by someone else. The spark, the independence, the person you knew, all seem to have vanished. What remains is someone who exists in service to the relationship and cannot imagine any alternative.

For men especially, Stage One often presents as calm, rational, or "fine." He is not safe. He has learned to minimise distress, suppress emotion, and cope silently because that is what he believes a man is supposed to do.

The Dynamic

Understanding what is happening (both what she is doing and what he is experiencing internally) helps explain why this stage looks the way it does.

What She Is Doing

In Stage One, the control system is fully operational. She has successfully installed her framework as his primary lens for interpreting reality, and she maintains it through continuous reinforcement.

- **Isolation maintenance.** She ensures that outside perspectives remain limited. This might be overt ("Your family doesn't really care about you") or subtle (scheduling conflicts that make family contact difficult, expressing displeasure after visits that makes him reluctant to repeat them). The goal is ensuring her voice is the dominant one in his life.

- **Reality control.** She defines what events mean. When something happens, her interpretation is presented as objective truth. His alternative interpretations are dismissed, mocked, or met with consequences that train him to stop offering them. Eventually, he stops forming independent interpretations at all.

- **Intermittent reinforcement.** Periods of warmth and affection alternate unpredictably with criticism, coldness, or punishment. This pattern creates intense attachment, the good times feel precious

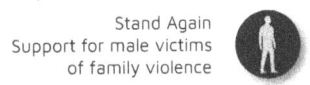

because they're surrounded by uncertainty, and he works constantly to produce them.

- **Identity erosion.** His sense of himself as an independent person with valid needs and perspectives is under continuous assault. Criticism of his character, dismissal of his feelings, and the requirement that he continuously prioritise her needs all contribute to a diminished sense of self.

- **Narrative construction.** She is actively constructing a story about who he is (flawed, lucky to have her), who she is (reasonable, long-suffering), and who everyone else is (unsupportive, jealous, hostile). This narrative, repeated constantly, becomes his reality.

What He Is Experiencing

Inside his experience, things look very different from how they appear to you.

- **He believes he is in a normal, if challenging, relationship.** The gradual nature of the control means he has no clear before-and-after to compare. This is just how relationships are. Yes, it's hard, but all relationships require work.

- **He believes the problems are his fault.** He has absorbed her narrative that he is the one failing to meet reasonable expectations. If he were just more attentive, more understanding, better at anticipating her needs: things would be fine. His constant failure to achieve this proves his inadequacy.

- **He is exhausted.** The effort of constantly monitoring her mood, managing her reactions, and suppressing his own needs is draining. But he may not recognise this exhaustion as caused by the relationship: it's just how life feels.

- **He loves her.** The trauma bond creates genuine feelings of love and attachment. The person harming him is also the person he is most bonded to. This is not confusion or stupidity: It is the predictable neurological result of intermittent reinforcement.

- **His authentic self is buried but not destroyed.** Somewhere beneath the adapted self that manages the relationship is the person he was before. This authentic self may surface occasionally: a flash of the old humour, a moment of genuine connection before being suppressed again.

- **For men specifically: his sense of masculine failure compounds everything.** He may feel he is failing as a man. Failing to make his partner happy, failing to maintain a successful relationship, failing to be strong and in control. This shame reinforces his silence. Admitting problems would mean admitting to failures that strike at his identity.

This is also where the Blueprint of Family Violence Against Men becomes useful for families. Understanding the specific tactics being used on him helps explain why his internal world looks nothing like his external presentation. His withdrawal, flatness, defensiveness, or rehearsed explanations are not apathy. They're adaptations. When families misinterpret these adaptations as "his personality now," they underestimate the severity of the trap.

What He Needs / What to Avoid

What He Needs

- **Continued connection without agenda.** He needs to know you exist, that you love him, and that contact with you is pleasant rather than fraught. This means interactions that are warm and relatively light. Not interrogations, not expressions of concern, not attempts to open his eyes.

- **A relationship that feels different from his primary one.** His experience with her is characterised by conditionality, criticism, and unpredictability. Your relationship can offer the opposite: unconditional acceptance, warmth, and consistency. This contrast plants seeds, even if he cannot consciously recognise it.

- **Connection to his pre-relationship identity.** Engaging with interests he had before the relationship, shared memories, aspects of his

identity that are independent of her: these keep the authentic self accessible, even if buried.

- **The absence of pressure.** He already lives under constant pressure. Adding more pressure from another direction does not liberate him; it makes contact with you feel like another performance to manage. Be a refuge, not another demand.

What to Avoid

- **Criticising her.** At this stage, he cannot hear criticism of her as anything other than an attack on him and his choices. Every criticism strengthens his defence of the relationship and confirms her narrative that his family is hostile.

- **Presenting evidence of abuse.** He is not ready to process this. The psychological structures that prevent him from seeing the abuse will filter out or reinterpret any evidence you present. Save this for later stages, if it's ever appropriate at all.

- **Expressing frequent concern.** Occasional, gentle expressions of care are fine. Repeated expressions of worry become pressure. "I'm always here for you" is enough. You don't need to say it every time you speak.

- **Forcing him to choose.** Any situation that becomes "us or her" will likely resolve in her favour, and you will have lost access entirely. Keep the door open; don't force him through it before he's ready.

If You've Already Made Mistakes

Many parents find this book after they have already said or done things they now regret. You may have criticised her directly. Issued ultimatums. Told him exactly what you think of his relationship. Perhaps you did this years ago. Perhaps last week.

The damage from past approaches is real, but it is rarely irreversible.

- **Acknowledge what you did, briefly and without drama.** "I know I said some things about your relationship that weren't helpful. I'm sorry. I was worried about you, but that's not an excuse." One acknowledgment is enough. Repeated apologies become a new form of pressure.

- **Change your behaviour, not just your words.** An apology followed by the same patterns means nothing. If you said you'd stop criticising and then criticise again next month, the apology is erased.

- **Accept that trust takes time to rebuild.** He may be wary of you. He may expect the old patterns to resurface. The only way to prove you've changed is through sustained, different behaviour.

- **Forgive yourself.** You were trying to help someone you love. The approaches that backfired were driven by care, even if they were counterproductive. Carrying guilt does not help him or you.

With male victims, wariness can often look like indifference rather than hurt. Don't mistake emotional flatness for lack of impact. He may feel the relationship rupture deeply; men simply learned not to show it.

Specific Scenarios You May Encounter

When You've Been Estranged

Some parents come to this book after months or years of estrangement. The relationship has already been severed. He doesn't answer calls, doesn't respond to messages, doesn't attend family gatherings. You may only now be understanding that this estrangement wasn't really his choice.

Estrangement in coercive control relationships typically has one of two origins: she has engineered it, or your previous attempts to help drove him away. Often, both.

The goal now is re-establishing any contact at all. This requires patience and a different approach than maintaining existing connection.

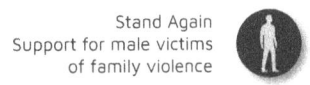

- **Low-stakes outreach.** Brief, warm messages with no expectation of response. "Thinking of you today. Hope you're well." A birthday text. A holiday greeting. These establish that you exist, that you're not angry, that the door is open.

- **No pressure, no guilt.** "We never see you anymore" or "Your grandmother keeps asking about you" weaponises other relationships and creates exactly the kind of pressure that makes contact less likely.

- **Accept non-response.** He may not respond for a long time. Each message you send still registers somewhere. He knows you reached out. The absence of response does not mean the absence of impact.

- **If she monitors his communication** (and she probably does), your messages should be entirely benign. Nothing she could use as evidence of hostility. Nothing that creates conflict for him.

The timeline for re-establishing contact after estrangement is measured in months and years, not weeks. Consistency matters more than frequency. One message every month for two years builds a foundation that twenty messages in a month does not.

When Silence Stretches Into Years

There is a particular weight to sending messages that receive no reply. Week after week. Month after month. Year after year. You are speaking into silence, with no evidence that your words land anywhere.

This is one of the loneliest positions a parent can occupy. You are maintaining love for someone who gives you nothing back. You are investing in a relationship that, from all visible evidence, may no longer exist.

Some guidance for sustaining this:

- **Find a rhythm you can maintain indefinitely.** One message a month is more sustainable than weekly contact that burns you out after six months. Choose a frequency that feels manageable even if this continues for years, because it might. Vary the content lightly. A birthday message. A photo of something that reminded you of him. A brief note saying you were thinking of him. You do not need to say anything profound. The message is the message: "I am here. I have not forgotten you".

- **Do not escalate when you get no response.** The temptation is to increase frequency or emotional intensity. To write longer messages. To plead. This rarely helps and may make things worse. Steady and calm. That is what cuts through.

- **Manage your own hope carefully.** Each message you send can become a small hope that this will be the one he responds to. When he does not, the disappointment accumulates. Try to send messages without attachment to response. You are maintaining a thread. Whether he picks it up is not something you control.

- **Keep a record for yourself.** Some parents find it helpful to keep copies of what they send. Not for evidence, but for their own sanity. On dark days, you can look back and see: I have not abandoned him. I have been here, consistently, even when it cost me.

The silence may break suddenly. When it does, it often comes without warning. A text. A call. A request to meet. You want to be someone who has been consistent, not someone who gave up or whose last message was angry or guilt-laden. The thread you are maintaining may be the one he eventually pulls.

When She Is Actively Blocking Access

Sometimes the problem isn't that he won't respond. It's that she is actively preventing contact. Calls are answered by her. Messages are deleted before he sees them. Invitations are declined on his behalf. She speaks for him, manages his relationships, controls who has access.

This is one of the most painful positions to be in as a parent. You are watching your son disappear behind a wall she has constructed.

What You Can Do

- **Find channels she doesn't control.** Does he have a work email? An old social media account she may not monitor? Are there moments when he is physically away from her: work trips, visits to other relatives? These may offer windows for contact she cannot block.

- **Use intermediaries *carefully*.** A sibling, cousin, or friend who still has access may be able to carry messages or provide connection. But choose intermediaries carefully. They must understand the situation and be discreet.

- **Don't fight her directly.** Confronting her about blocking access will likely escalate things. She may tighten control further. Your goal is maintaining whatever connection is possible, not winning battles.

Document The Blocking

Keep records of calls not returned, messages not answered, invitations declined on his behalf. Note dates, times, and what occurred. Save screenshots where possible. This documentation serves several purposes.

- First, it **helps you maintain clarity.** When you can see the pattern laid out, you are less likely to doubt your own perception.

- Second, it **may help him later**. If he leaves and faces a custody dispute, evidence of her pattern of isolating him from support systems becomes relevant. Evidence of her blocking his family's access to the children becomes relevant. You are not building a case against her. You are preparing to support him if he ever needs it.

- Third, it **creates a timeline he may need**. When he emerges, he may struggle to reconstruct what happened and when. Your records can help him understand the full picture. Keep documentation factual and minimal. Dates, brief descriptions, evidence where available. This is not a place to process your emotions or build an argument. It is a simple record of what occurred.

Do not become obsessive about this. Document enough to have a clear record. Do not let documentation become a substitute for living your own life.

What You Cannot Do

You cannot force access to an adult child.

This is one of the hardest truths of this situation. If he is an adult, and if he (under her influence) does not want contact, you have no legal recourse to demand it. You cannot sue for access to your adult son. You cannot petition a court to intervene. His autonomy, even when that autonomy is being manipulated, is protected.

Accepting this lack of control is not giving up. It is recognising reality. Your power lies in persistence, in continuing to exist, continuing to reach out, continuing to make clear that the door remains open whenever he is able to walk through it.

When You Cannot Reach Your Grandchildren

If there are grandchildren you cannot see, this grief compounds everything. You are losing not only your son but his children. They are growing up without you. Milestones pass unmarked. You do not know what they look like, what they are interested in, who they are becoming.

There are things you can do, even from exile: Create an email address for each grandchild. Write to them. Not constantly, but regularly. Tell them about yourself. Share family history. Describe their father as a child. Attach photos. They cannot read these emails now, but someday they may be old enough to search for you. When they do, they will find an archive of love waiting. Build a scrapbook or memory box. Photos of their father growing up. Family documents. Letters explaining who you are and how much you wanted to know them. A record of the family they were kept from.

When reunion becomes possible, this becomes a gift. Evidence that they were thought of, missed, and loved even in absence. Document significant dates. Birthdays, holidays, milestones you imagine they are reaching. Write a note for each one, even if you cannot send it. "Today you turn seven. I hope you are happy. I love you."

This may feel futile. You are creating things that may never be seen, writing to children who do not know you exist. But you are also preparing for a future that may come. Children grow up. They ask questions. They search for family.

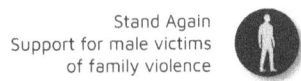

You want to be findable. You want them to discover, when they look, that you were here all along. If they do reach out someday, what they will need is not a grandparent who is bitter about lost years. They will need someone who can welcome them without burdening them with the full weight of what happened.

The scrapbook, the emails, the documented love. These give you somewhere to put the grief now so that when the moment comes, you can simply be present.

When She Has Poisoned Your Reputation

She has told him you are the problem. Controlling. Toxic. Narcissistic. A bad influence. The reason their relationship is difficult. The enemy of their happiness.

These narratives serve her purposes: they justify isolation from you, they create defensiveness in him if you try to help, and they provide an external enemy that distracts from the internal dynamics of the relationship.

He may have absorbed these narratives. He may believe them, or half-believe them, or feel confused about what is true.

Responding to the Smear Campaign

- **Do not defend yourself aggressively.** This confirms her narrative that you are combative and reactive. "I'm sorry you've been told that. It's not how I see things, but I understand if you're unsure about me right now." This neither concedes the point nor escalates conflict.

- **Let your behaviour speak.** If she says you're controlling, be consistently non-controlling. If she says you're critical, be consistently accepting. If she says you're dramatic, be consistently calm. Behaviour over time is more persuasive than arguments.

- **Don't fight her narrative directly to him.** Saying "She's lying about me" puts him in the middle and forces him to choose whose version of reality to believe. He is not ready for that choice.

- **Manage the wider narrative carefully.** She may spread her version to mutual acquaintances, extended family, or community connections. You can correct misinformation when directly asked, but avoid initiating a counter-campaign. Restraint reads as credibility.

The hardest part is that her narrative may contain distortions of real events. Perhaps you did say something critical. Perhaps you were worried and expressed it too strongly. She takes a kernel of truth and builds a false structure around it. You cannot easily refute the kernel without engaging with the whole false structure.

Hold onto this: he knew you before her. Whatever false narrative she constructs exists in tension with years of experience. The narrative may hold sway now, while he is in her orbit. It becomes less credible as distance grows.

When People in Your Life Cannot See It

Not everyone who doubts you is a flying monkey. Some people in your life genuinely cannot see what you see. They have met her. She was lovely. They cannot reconcile the charming woman who brought wine to dinner with the person you are describing.

This is disorienting. You begin to wonder if you are the one who is wrong. If you are seeing things that are not there. If your concern has become obsession.

Some context: Abusers are often exceptionally skilled at public presentation. The warmth, the attentiveness, the apparent devotion to your son. This is not an act she puts on occasionally. It is a carefully maintained facade that only drops behind closed doors. The people in your life are not stupid for being fooled. They are seeing exactly what she wants them to see.

When friends or extended family express doubt: You do not need to convince them. Attempting to build a case, present evidence, or argue your position typically exhausts you and rarely changes minds. People believe what they see, and what they see is the public face.

Share selectively. Some people in your life will be able to hold complexity. Others will not. Learn who can hear this and who cannot. Protect your energy for the people who can actually support you.

Name what you need. "I'm not asking you to agree with my assessment. I'm asking you to trust that I'm not making this up and to support me even if you're not sure."

Sometimes people can offer support without full belief. That may be enough. Accept that some relationships may strain. People who actively argue that you are wrong, who defend her, who suggest you are the problem. These relationships may need distance.

You cannot carry their doubt alongside everything else. Find people who understand. Support groups, online communities, others who have watched someone they love disappear into a controlling relationship. These people will not need convincing. They will recognise what you describe immediately. Your perception is not invalidated by others' inability to see. You know your son. You have watched the change.

The fact that she performs well in public does not make your observations false.

Managing Your Own Reactions

Watching Stage One unfold is excruciating. Every instinct screams at you to do something. The urge to shake him awake, to force him to see, to rescue him from what you can clearly perceive: this urge is constant and powerful.

Managing your reactions is not about suppression. It's about having somewhere to put them that isn't him.

When He Defends Her

You make a mild observation - he looks tired, perhaps - and suddenly he's explaining how hard she works and how much she does for him. The defence seems disproportionate, rehearsed, robotic.

Inside, you want to scream.

What helps: understanding that his defence is not really about you. He is managing his own cognitive dissonance. He is reciting the framework that lets him function. Arguing with the defence reinforces it. Accepting it without agreement lets the moment pass.

"I'm glad you have each other's support" is enough. You haven't conceded the point. You've simply declined to fight about it.

When He Parrots Her Views About You

He expresses opinions about you, about the family, about past events, that sound exactly like her. The words coming out of his mouth are not his words. You are talking to her ventriloquism.

This can trigger rage, grief, or both.

It is painful, but remember: he is repeating narratives that men often adopt when they feel ashamed - distancing, intellectualising, and defending the person who hurt them rather than admitting vulnerability.

- **What helps:** recognising that your son is still in there. The adapted self who parrots her views is a survival mechanism, not a replacement. He is saying what he needs to say to function in his current reality. When that reality changes, so will what he says.

When He Minimises

"It's not that bad." "You're overreacting." "She's just stressed." "Every relationship has rough patches." When he minimises, he is not lying to you. He is managing his own cognitive dissonance. If it is "not that bad," he does not have to confront what it actually is. The minimisation protects him from a truth he is not ready to face.

Responses that neither agree nor escalate: "I hear you. I hope things ease up for you." "That makes sense. I'm still here if you ever want to talk." "I'm glad it feels manageable. You know where I am if that changes." "Okay. Just know I'm always in your corner."

- **What you are doing**: acknowledging what he said without endorsing it, leaving the door open without pushing through it. You are not agreeing that everything is fine. You are also not arguing.

- **What to avoid**: "That's not what it looks like from here." "You always say that." "When are you going to see what's really happening?" These responses feel honest but they close the conversation and put him on the defensive.

The goal is to be someone he can come to when the minimisation stops working. That requires not being someone he associates with pressure, argument, or "I told you so." Absorb the minimisation. Let it pass. Stay warm. Stay present. When the cracks form, he will remember who made it safe to speak.

When He Seems Like a Stranger

The person in front of you bears little resemblance to the son you raised. His values seem different. His personality seems flattened. The spark is gone. You find yourself grieving someone who is technically still alive.

This is perhaps the deepest pain of Stage One.

- **What helps**: understanding that this stranger-self is adaptive camouflage, not permanent transformation. The person you knew developed those qualities in an environment that supported them. The current environment requires different qualities for survival. Given a different environment, different qualities can re-emerge.

- **What also helps**: letting yourself grieve. You are experiencing a loss, even if it's ambiguous and potentially temporary. Suppressing the grief makes it harder to be present with him. Acknowledging it: to yourself, to your partner, to a therapist creates room to function.

When Navigating Family Events

Holidays, birthdays, weddings, funerals these events concentrate the difficulty of Stage One. Everyone is together. Expectations run high. She is likely present. The gap between how things should be and how they are becomes impossible to ignore.

When She Controls His Attendance

He may skip events, arriving late and leaving early if he comes at all. His attendance may depend on her mood, her willingness to accompany him, or manufactured conflicts that prevent him from coming. Last-minute cancellations become a pattern.

You cannot make him come. You can make coming feel as easy and pressure-free as possible.

"We'd love to see you if you can make it. No pressure either way." This is the right tone. Disappointment when he doesn't show, while natural, should be expressed minimally and without guilt-tripping.

When He Cancels Plans at the Last Minute

This is common in Stage One. She may create conflicts, express displeasure about his plans, or manufacture crises that require him to stay. He cancels, often with an excuse that sounds thin.

Your response: mild disappointment is appropriate, but avoid guilt-tripping or demanding explanations. Something like "I'm sorry to miss you. Let's find another time" keeps the door open. Expressing anger or hurt, while natural, may make him more reluctant to try making plans in the future.

She Accompanies Him to All Family Events

You may notice he never comes alone anymore. She is present at every gathering, often monitoring conversations or steering him away from extended private chats with family members.

Your response: accept her presence without comment. Attempting to exclude her or create opportunities for him to be alone will likely be reported back and used as evidence of family hostility. Be pleasant to her. Endure. You are playing a long game.

Managing Other Family Members

Extended family may not understand the situation. Aunts, uncles, grandparents may ask pointed questions, make comments, or confront him or her directly. Well-meaning relatives can undo careful work with a single thoughtless remark.

Brief family members in advance when possible. "We're keeping things light. No questions about the relationship." Not everyone will comply, but setting expectations helps.

If someone does create a scene, don't compound it. Smooth things over, move on, and assess damage later.

When He Announces an Engagement or Pregnancy

This is devastating to hear when you believe the relationship is abusive. The formalisation of the relationship or the addition of children seems to close doors and deepen his entrapment.

Your response: respond as you would if you had no concerns - with appropriate congratulations. This is not the moment to voice objections. Objecting will not stop the engagement or pregnancy; it will only damage your relationship with him. Stay close. You will be needed more than ever, and you cannot be needed if you have been cut off.

Preparing for Years, Not Months

Stage One can last a very long time.

Months. Years. In some cases, decades. The psychological structures that keep someone trapped in a coercive control relationship are robust. They do not collapse quickly or easily. External pressure typically reinforces rather than weakens them.

This is not failure. Yours or his. It is the nature of the trap.

Preparing yourself for a long timeline means:

- **Sustainability over intensity.** You cannot maintain crisis-level engagement for years. Finding a sustainable level of concern (present but not consuming) is essential for your survival.

- **Releasing attachment to timelines.** "Surely by next year..." becomes "I don't know when or if." This is painful but necessary. Hope tied to specific timelines crashes repeatedly; hope without timeline can persist.

- **Measuring success differently.** If success means "he leaves," you may never feel successful. If success means "I maintained connection and remained available," you can experience success even while waiting.

- **Living your own life.** Your life cannot be on hold indefinitely. Work, friendships, interests, your relationship with your partner, your other children. These continue and deserve attention regardless of his situation.

The timeline is not in your control. What you do within that timeline is.

Positioning for Movement

You cannot push him from Stage One to Stage Two. But you can maintain conditions that make his eventual movement more likely and ensure you are positioned to be helpful when it happens.

Important: The suggestions in this section are about positioning, not pushing. They carry risk of backfiring if applied with too much force or frequency. When in doubt, prioritise maintaining connection over attempting to create openings.

- **Remain present and accessible.** Whatever happens, he should know at a deep level that you exist and can be reached. Regular contact, even if brief and surface-level, maintains this awareness.

- **Model healthy relationships.** Your relationship with your spouse, your other family members, your friends - these provide contrast to his primary relationship. He may not consciously compare, but the differences register somewhere.

- **Engage with his pre-relationship self.** Bring up old interests, shared memories, aspects of identity that existed before her. "Remember when you used to..." can reconnect him to parts of himself that have been suppressed, without directly criticising the relationship.

- **Plant occasional seeds.** Very occasionally, a gentle observation or question can be offered: "You seem tired lately. Everything okay?" These are not interventions. They are invitations that he can decline. If he deflects, let it go. The seed is planted; whether it takes root is not in your control.

    Be patient with the long timeline. Stage One can last years. Your job during this time is not to create movement but to maintain the conditions under which movement becomes possible when he's ready.

KEY TAKEAWAYS:

- **STAGE ONE IS ABOUT SURVIVAL - YOURS AND HIS.**

- **HE CANNOT YET SEE THAT ANYTHING IS WRONG.**

- **YOUR JOB IS NOT TO OPEN HIS EYES - THAT WILL FAIL - BUT TO REMAIN PRESENT, WARM, AND CONNECTED SO THAT WHEN THE INTERNAL PROCESS OF RECOGNITION BEGINS, YOU ARE POSITIONED TO MATTER.**

- **IF YOU'VE MADE MISTAKES, YOU CAN RECOVER.**

- **IF YOU'VE BEEN ESTRANGED, YOU CAN REBUILD.**

- **IF SHE'S BLOCKING ACCESS, YOU CAN PERSIST.**

- **IF SHE'S POISONED YOUR REPUTATION, YOU CAN LET BEHAVIOUR SPEAK.**

- **THE TIMELINE MAY BE LONG. PREPARE ACCORDINGLY.**

Chapter 8: Stage Two - Cracks Forming

In this stage, the solid wall of denial begins to develop cracks. Something is shifting internally. He may not name it or acknowledge it, but moments of doubt are surfacing. These cracks are fragile. Handled carefully, they may widen. Handled clumsily, they may seal back up.

Recognising This Stage

Stage Two is subtle. From outside, the situation may look identical to Stage One. The differences are internal, occasionally surfacing in small ways that are easy to miss if you're not watching carefully.

Signs that cracks may be forming:

- **He occasionally acknowledges problems** in the relationship, even if he quickly reframes them or takes all the blame.

- **His defences of her seem less automatic,** more effortful: as though he's convincing himself as much as you.

- **He asks questions** that suggest internal conflict: "Is this normal?" "Did you and Dad go through phases like this?"

- **He seems to be seeking connection** with you more than before: calling more often, staying longer at visits, seeming reluctant to leave.

- **He shows flashes of his old self**: humour, opinions, preferences before quickly returning to the more guarded persona.

- **He makes small complaints** that he would not have voiced before, even if followed by qualifications.

- **His exhaustion seems closer to the surface**: he looks worn down in ways that are harder to hide.

These signs are tentative. Men often stay in Stage Two longer than families expect because doubt itself feels like failure. He may "try harder" at the relationship during this phase, not because it's working but because he believes he must prove his worth before admitting something is wrong.

He may be in Stage Two for a conversation and seemingly back in Stage One by the next. The cracks form and then fill in; they form again in different places. This is not regression but the normal pattern of an internal process that advances unevenly.

The Dynamic

What She Is Doing

She may or may not sense the internal shift. If she does, she will intensify efforts to maintain control.

- **Increased monitoring.** She may become more watchful of his communications, his movements, his emotional state. His access to you may become more restricted.

- **Strategic warmth.** She may respond to sensed distance with increased affection, reminding him of why he loves her and why the relationship is worth preserving. This can be confusing for him and for you. Things seem better, so perhaps there was never a problem.

- **Escalated consequences.** Alternatively, she may escalate punishment for signs of independence or outside connection. The message is clear: questioning the relationship comes with costs.

- **Creating crises.** Manufactured emergencies: health scares, financial problems, family conflicts can redirect his attention back to the relationship and away from his forming doubts.

What He Is Experiencing

Stage Two is characterised by cognitive dissonance in flux. The framework that explained everything is developing gaps, but no alternative framework has taken its place.

- **Confusion.** Things that used to make sense don't quite fit anymore. Her explanations for events sometimes feel inadequate. He may experience this as fog: a sense that something is off without clarity about what.

- **Guilt about doubting.** He has been trained to see doubt as disloyalty. Questioning the relationship feels like betraying her, and the guilt this produces may push him back toward full acceptance.

- **Longing for the outside.** He may find himself thinking about life outside the relationship. About old friends, old interests, other ways things could be. These thoughts may feel dangerous and need to be suppressed.

- **Testing the waters.** He may tentatively test outside relationships, reaching out more than before, staying in conversations longer, perhaps even hinting at difficulties. These tests help him gauge whether the outside world is as hostile as she has portrayed it.

For men specifically: the shame of admitting anything is wrong remains powerful. Even as doubts form, he may be unable to voice them because doing so would require acknowledging that his relationship is not what he has claimed. That he, a man, is not in control of his own life.

What He Needs / What to Avoid

What He Needs

- **A safe place to think.** His internal process needs space. Time with you that is low-pressure and accepting provides room for thoughts he cannot think at home.

- **Validation without pushing.** If he expresses a doubt or acknowledges a problem, your response should validate what he's shared without escalating to conclusions he's not ready for. "That sounds hard" rather than "See, I told you she was abusing you."

- **Questions that invite reflection.** Open-ended questions that help him think, without pushing particular answers: "How did that feel?" "What do you think about that?" "What would make things better?" These questions honour his capacity to think for himself.

- **Continued unconditional presence.** The cracks forming make this stage fragile. He needs to know that you will be there regardless of what he concludes - whether he decides to stay, leave, or continue in uncertainty indefinitely.

What to Avoid

- **Pouncing on the cracks.** When he admits something is wrong, the temptation to capitalise on the opening is overwhelming. But pushing too hard at this stage often causes the cracks to seal up. He retreats into defence, and the opening closes.

- **Naming things before he does.** He may be experiencing abuse without being able to use that word. Forcing terminology on him before he's ready can trigger rejection of the entire framework. Let him find his own language.

- **Expressing relief or excitement.** If he seems to be waking up, your visible relief may feel like pressure. It signals that you have an investment in his conclusion, which can make him feel manipulated rather than supported.

- **Providing ultimatums or timelines.** "Now that you see it, you need to leave" is not helpful. He is at the beginning of a process, not the end. Demanding action before he's ready can set everything back.

Specific Scenarios You May Encounter

He Makes a Small Complaint

"She's been really stressed lately and taking it out on me." This is a significant moment. He is acknowledging something is wrong, even while minimising it.

Your response: listen carefully. Reflect back what he's said: "That sounds frustrating." Ask how he's coping. Do not escalate ("That's not stress, that's abuse") or minimise ("All couples go through that"). Hold space for his experience as he's describing it.

He Asks for Advice About the Relationship

"How do you and Dad handle it when you disagree?" Questions like this suggest he's looking for reference points, possibly because his internal compass is recalibrating.

Your response: answer honestly but without pointed comparison. Describe how healthy relationships work, using your own experience as illustration. Avoid "Unlike her, your father..." framing. Let him draw his own conclusions about how his relationship compares.

He Seems to Be Testing Your Reaction

He shares something concerning and then watches your response carefully. He may be gauging whether it's safe to share more, or whether outside perspectives will be as harsh as he fears.

Your response: stay calm and supportive. Don't overreact with alarm or anger, which may confirm that sharing is dangerous. Don't underreact with dismissal. Strike a middle ground: caring, present, non-judgmental. "Thank you for telling me. I'm here for you."

He Seems Better - Has She Changed?

After a period of visible tension, things suddenly seem improved. He seems happier, less guarded, more like his old self. Maybe she really has changed?

You may also notice emotional flatness instead of improvement: a blankness that wasn't present before. This isn't regression; it's a protective shutdown while his internal landscape reconfigures.

Your response: this may be genuine improvement, or it may be the "honeymoon phase" of the abuse cycle: a period of strategic warmth designed to rebuild his investment. You cannot know from outside. Accept the

improvement without celebrating it as resolution. Remain present. If the pattern is cyclical, it will repeat.

Positioning for Movement

Stage Two offers more opportunities for careful engagement than Stage One, but the same cautions apply: positioning, not pushing.

Important: The openings in Stage Two are fragile. Overplaying your hand can close them. Err on the side of too little rather than too much.

- **Listen more than you speak.** When he shares, your primary job is to receive, not to respond with your own perspective. Ask questions. Reflect back what you hear. Create space for him to continue thinking.

- **Normalise his confusion.** He may feel he should have clear answers. Let him know it's okay to be uncertain. "It makes sense that you're confused. These things are complicated."

- **Offer resources obliquely.** If appropriate, you might mention something you've read or heard about relationships. Not as pointed commentary on his situation, but as something interesting. "I was reading about how couples handle stress..." He can choose whether to apply it to himself.

- **Maintain connection without intensity.** The goal remains ongoing presence. Don't let the excitement of possible movement lead you to intensify contact in ways that feel like pressure or surveillance.

- **Prepare for regression.** He may move from Stage Two back to Stage One. If this happens, it is not failure - yours or his. It is the normal pattern of change. Continue leaving the light on.

KEY TAKEAWAY:

- **STAGE TWO IS FRAGILE – CRACKS ARE FORMING, BUT THEY CAN SEAL UP AGAIN.**

- **YOUR ROLE IS TO PROVIDE A SAFE SPACE FOR HIS EMERGING DOUBTS WITHOUT PUSHING CONCLUSIONS HE'S NOT READY FOR.**

- **LISTEN, VALIDATE, HOLD SPACE, AND RESIST THE URGE TO CAPITALISE ON OPENINGS.**

- **MOVEMENT AT THIS STAGE COMES FROM INSIDE HIM, NOT FROM OUTSIDE PRESSURE.**

Chapter 9: Stage Three - Crisis Point

Something has happened that cannot be explained away. The internal structure of denial has collapsed or is collapsing. He may be in acute distress. This is a pivotal moment and a dangerous one. How the crisis is handled shapes what comes next.

Recognising This Stage

Stage Three is often precipitated by an event: an escalation of abuse, a betrayal, a moment of clarity that cannot be unseen. The slow internal process of Stage Two has reached a tipping point.

Signs of a crisis point:

- **He reaches out to you with unusual urgency**: a phone call at an odd hour, a text asking to talk.

- **He discloses something significant about the relationship**: acknowledging abuse, admitting fear, expressing a desire to leave.

- **He appears in visible distress**: crying, shaking, unable to maintain his usual composure.

- **He asks for concrete help**: a place to stay, money, legal advice.

- **He uses language he has never used before**: "I can't do this anymore," "I think I need to get out," "Something is really wrong."

This moment may come after years of waiting, or it may come suddenly, before you expected it. Either way, it is critical and it may not last. The window that opens can close again.

The Dynamic

What She Is Doing

If she senses the crisis, she will deploy every tool available to prevent his exit.

- **Extreme remorse and promises to change.** She may become tearful, apologetic, and make seemingly sincere commitments to do things differently. "I know I've been hard on you. I'll get help. Please don't give up on us."

- **Threats.** She may threaten to harm herself, to destroy him financially or legally, to take the children, to ruin his reputation. These threats are designed to make leaving feel more dangerous than staying.

- **Mobilising others.** She may contact family, friends, or other connections to present her version of events, recruit allies, or create pressure on him to reconcile.

- **Using children.** If children are involved, she may weaponise them: threatening to limit access, involving them in the conflict, or using them as emotional leverage.

What He Is Experiencing

Stage Three is overwhelming. The psychological structures that made his life make sense have crumbled, and nothing has yet replaced them.

- **Terror.** Leaving, or even contemplating leaving, may feel genuinely life-threatening. This is not irrational. The period of leaving is statistically the most dangerous time in abusive relationships. His nervous system is responding to genuine threat.

- **Grief.** He may be mourning the relationship, the life he thought he had, the future he imagined. This grief is real, even if the relationship was harmful.

- **Confusion about reality.** With his framework collapsed, he may struggle to know what is true. Her narrative and the emerging truth are in conflict, and he may not know which to trust.

- **Shame.** The full weight of what has happened may be hitting him. Admitting to others and to himself what his life has actually been like is excruciating.

- **Ambivalence.** Even in crisis, he may feel pulled back toward her. The trauma bond does not dissolve in a moment of clarity. Part of him may still want to return, to make it work, to believe her promises.

- **For men specifically: the crisis may threaten his entire identity.** He is confronting a relationship crisis and a crisis of masculinity simultaneously. Everything he was supposed to be: strong, capable, in control feels like a lie. The shame can be paralysing.

What He Needs / What to Avoid

What He Needs

- **Immediate, practical support.** If he has reached out for help, provide it. A safe place to stay, help with logistics, whatever concrete assistance he needs. This is not the time for "I told you so" or for processing emotions. Action first.

- **Calm presence.** Your stability matters. He is in crisis. You need to be grounded. Even if you are feeling intense emotions, regulate yourself. He needs a grounded person to orient toward.

- **Non-judgmental listening.** He may need to talk a lot. Let him. Don't correct, debate, or redirect. The processing he needs to do will happen through talking, and it will happen on his timeline.

- **Affirmation of his worth.** His sense of self is shattered. Remind him of who he is beyond this relationship: his qualities, his strengths, his value as a person.

- **Safety planning if needed.** If there is any risk of violence or retaliation, safety needs to be addressed concretely. This may mean involving professionals.

- **Exit planning.** If exit is imminent or underway, detailed planning matters. Stand Again provides exit planning templates at standagain.com.au, including practical checklists and guidance for navigating the most dangerous phase of leaving.

What to Avoid

- **"I told you so."** However tempting, however true, this response shames him when he is already drowning in shame. It confirms that disclosure leads to humiliation and makes it less likely he will turn to you again if he falters.

- **Demanding immediate decisions.** He may not be ready to commit to leaving permanently. Forcing a binary choice: stay or go before he has processed what is happening can push him back toward the relationship.

- **Vilifying her extensively.** He is still attached to her. Extensive attacks on her character can feel like attacks on him, on his judgment, on his love. Focus on his experience and his needs rather than on her failures.

- **Expecting linear progress.** This crisis may resolve in departure or it may resolve in return to the relationship. Be prepared for either. If he returns, keep the door open.

Specific Scenarios You May Encounter

He Calls in Acute Distress

The phone rings, and he's crying, or speaking rapidly, or eerily calm in a way that signals shock. Something has happened, and he doesn't know what to do.

Your response: stay calm. Assess immediate safety first: "Are you safe right now? Is anyone hurt?" If safety is established, let him talk. Don't rush to solutions. "I'm here. Tell me what happened." If he needs to come to you, make that happen. Logistics can be figured out later.

He Shows Up at Your Door

He appears without warning, bag in hand, looking shattered. He has left or at least, he has left for tonight.

Your response: let him in, literally and figuratively. Don't require explanations before providing shelter. "I'm so glad you're here. Come in." Practical needs first: food, rest, quiet. The conversation can happen when he's ready.

The First 72 Hours

When he leaves, the first three days are critical. Everything is raw. Nothing is settled. The risk of return is highest. Your role in these hours can shape what happens next.

- **Practical needs come first.** Does he have somewhere safe to sleep tonight? Does he have his phone, wallet, identification? Has he eaten? These questions matter before any conversation about what happened or what comes next.

- **Stabilise the body before processing the mind.** Create calm. He has just exited chaos. Your home, your presence, your voice should offer the opposite. No urgent questions. No family meetings. No flood of relatives wanting to see him. Quiet. Space. Rest. Let him lead. He may want to talk for hours. He may want silence. He may swing between both. Follow his cues. Your job is to be available, not to direct.

- **Expect adrenaline and crash.** The first day may see him wired, talking fast, making plans. The second or third day may bring collapse: exhaustion, tears, paralysis. Both are normal. Neither is permanent. Limit decisions. He does not need to decide about divorce, custody, finances, or the future right now. The only decisions that matter in the first 72 hours are immediate safety and basic needs. Everything else can wait.

- **Watch for contact from her.** She will likely reach out. Texts, calls, voicemails. She may show up. She may send others. He may feel pulled to respond. Do not police his phone, but be aware that her attempts to pull him back will be intense in these early hours.

Stand Again
Support for male victims
of family violence

- **Do not debrief him.** The full story can wait. He does not need to explain or justify his departure to you or anyone else. "You're here. That's what matters. We can talk about everything else when you're ready."

- **Hold your own emotions.** You may feel overwhelming relief, rage at her, grief for what he has endured. These are valid. They are also not his to carry right now. Find another outlet.

These 72 hours are about his stabilisation, not your catharsis. If he wavers, stay steady. "I understand this is hard. You don't have to decide anything right now. You can stay here as long as you need." No pressure. No disappointment. Just presence.

She Contacts You

His partner reaches out: perhaps to explain her side, to recruit you as an ally, to find out where he is, or to make threats.

Your response: minimal engagement. You do not need to argue, explain, or defend. "This is between you and him. I'm not going to discuss it." If she makes threats, document them but do not react. Do not reveal his location or plans. Protect him.

He Wavers About Going Back

After a day or two of clarity, he starts reconsidering. She has called. She has apologised. Maybe things can be different. Maybe he overreacted.

Your response: this is normal. Don't panic. Don't issue ultimatums ("If you go back, I'm done"). Express your concern calmly: "I understand you still love her. I'm worried about you being safe. Whatever you decide, I'm here." If he returns, keep the door open for next time.

Positioning for Movement

Stage Three is the most active stage for your involvement, but "active" still means supporting rather than directing.

Important: Even in crisis, his agency matters. He is not a child to be rescued. He is an adult who needs support to make his own decisions. Guide, offer, assist - don't control.

- **Be ready with practical help.** Having thought in advance about what you can offer: space to stay, financial assistance, legal referrals means you can respond quickly when the moment comes.

- **Keep the focus on safety and immediate needs.** Long-term processing will happen later. Right now, what does he need today? Tonight? This week?

- **Connect him with professional resources.** Therapists, lawyers, domestic violence services (though these may be less available for men). You are not his only support, and you shouldn't be.

- **Prepare for return.** The first departure is often not the final one. Research suggests abuse victims leave multiple times before leaving for good. If he returns to her, this is not failure. It is the pattern. Your door remains open.

- **Manage your own emotions separately.** You will have intense feelings during this time. Process them with your partner, your therapist, your support system - not with him. He needs your stability, not your catharsis.

KEY TAKEAWAY:

- STAGE THREE IS A CRITICAL WINDOW.

- YOUR ROLE SHIFTS TO ACTIVE SUPPORT: PROVIDING PRACTICAL HELP, CALM PRESENCE, AND UNCONDITIONAL ACCEPTANCE.

- AVOID "I TOLD YOU SO" AND DEMANDS FOR IMMEDIATE DECISIONS.

- BE PREPARED FOR AMBIVALENCE AND POSSIBLE RETURN TO THE RELATIONSHIP.

- KEEP THE DOOR OPEN REGARDLESS OF WHAT HE DECIDES.

Chapter 10: Stage Four - Early Exit

He has left. The immediate crisis of Stage Three has given way to a new reality: life outside the relationship. This stage is marked by vulnerability, volatility, and the ongoing risk of return. The exit is not yet complete; it is still forming.

Recognising This Stage

Stage Four begins when he has physically separated from his partner but has not yet stabilised in a new life. This may last weeks or months.

Signs of early exit:

- **He is living separately from her**: with you, with friends, in his own place.

- **He oscillates between relief and grief**: sometimes within the same conversation.

- **He may still be in contact with her**: perhaps about logistics, children, or ongoing emotional entanglement.

- **He is beginning to process what happened**: but is still in early stages of understanding.

- **He may express doubt, guilt, or longing for the relationship**: the trauma bond is not yet broken.

- **Practical matters**: housing, finances, legal issues are in flux.

The Dynamic

What She Is Doing

Having failed to prevent the exit, she will now work to reverse it or to maintain whatever hold she can.

- **Hoovering.** The term, derived from the vacuum cleaner, describes attempts to suck him back in: apologies, promises, reminders of good times, appeals to shared history or commitment.

- **Weaponising children.** If children are involved, she may use them as leverage: limiting access, making him feel guilty for their distress, or involving them in adult conflicts.

- **Legal and financial attacks.** She may initiate legal proceedings, make false accusations, or take financial actions designed to punish him or force dependency.

- **Smear campaign.** She may tell others her version of events, painting herself as victim and him as abuser or abandoner. Mutual friends, his workplace, even his family may receive this narrative.

- **Harassment.** Continued contact: calls, texts, showing up unexpectedly. Designed to prevent him from establishing distance and processing what happened.

What He Is Experiencing

Withdrawal. The trauma bond operates somewhat like addiction. Being away from her creates genuine distress: anxiety, longing, a sense that something essential is missing. This is physiological as well as psychological.

- **Identity reconstruction.** Who is he outside this relationship? The adapted self was shaped by her; the authentic self is only beginning to re-emerge. He may feel uncertain about basic preferences and desires.

- **Grief and guilt.** He is grieving the relationship, the future he imagined, and possibly the version of her that he loved. He may feel

guilty for leaving, for "failing" to make it work, for any distress she or the children are experiencing.

- **Practical overwhelm.** The logistics of separation: housing, finances, custody, dividing possessions are exhausting and can consume all available mental and emotional resources.

- **Temptation to return.** The chaos of new life can make the known patterns of the old life feel appealing. At least in the relationship, he knew what to expect. The pull to go back is strong.

- **For men specifically: navigating systems that may not believe him.** Legal and social systems may view him with suspicion rather than support. He may face accusations of being the perpetrator rather than the victim. This compounds the difficulty of exit.

What He Needs / What to Avoid

What He Needs

- **Stability.** If he's staying with you, make it genuinely safe and stable. Not temporary, not conditional, not a place where he feels like a burden. He needs a foundation from which to rebuild.

- **Patience with his pace.** He may not be ready to fully process what happened. He may not be ready to be angry at her. He may still love her. Meet him where he is, not where you think he should be.

- **Practical help with logistics.** Help navigating the practical complexity of separation: finding housing, understanding legal options, managing finances. This concrete support matters.

- **Connection to professional support.** Encourage (but don't force) engagement with a therapist, counsellor, or support group. He has a lot to process, and you cannot be his only support.

- **Space for him to be him.** Encourage reconnection with old friends, old interests, aspects of himself that were suppressed. But don't push. Let him rediscover himself at his own pace.

What to Avoid

- **Expecting immediate healing.** He has just exited a traumatic situation. The healing will take much longer than the crisis. He may struggle, regress, and have bad days for a long time.

- **Surveillance of his contact with her.** He may still be in contact. This may be necessary (children, logistics) or it may be the trauma bond. Either way, monitoring and judging his contact creates another controlling dynamic. Trust him to figure it out.

- **Pushing him to "move on."** He is not ready to date. He is not ready to "put this behind him." Recovery is a process, not a decision. Pushing forward before he's ready can lead to new unhealthy relationships or incomplete processing.

- **Intense emotional reactions to his ambivalence.** When he expresses doubt or longing for her, your fear and frustration are natural. But expressing them intensely "How can you say that after what she did?" closes him down. He needs to be able to think out loud without judgment.

Specific Scenarios You May Encounter

He Is Still Talking to Her

You see texts on his phone. You hear phone calls. She is not out of his life, and this concerns you.

Your response: unless there is an immediate safety concern, avoid making this a point of conflict. You can observe that ongoing contact seems to be causing distress: "I notice you seem upset after talking to her. How are you doing?" But don't forbid or demand. He is an adult navigating a difficult transition.

He Says He Misses Her

"I know it was bad, but I still miss her." This statement may feel like betrayal of everything you've been through.

Your response: validate without encouraging return. "That makes sense. You loved her. You built a life together. Of course you miss parts of that." The trauma bond takes time to break. Missing her does not mean he should go back; it means he is human.

She Makes Accusations to Others

You hear through others that she is telling people he was the abuser, that he abandoned his family, that he is dangerous. The narrative she's spinning is the opposite of reality.

Your response: document but don't engage publicly. He may need to address this legally if it affects custody or his reputation. But arguing with her narrative in social circles typically makes things worse. People will draw their own conclusions based on behaviour over time.

He Returns to Her

After days or weeks of separation, he decides to go back. He believes she has changed, or believes he should try harder, or simply cannot tolerate the pain of separation.

Your response: this is heartbreaking, but it is his choice. Express your love and your concern without issuing ultimatums. "I'm worried about you, and I wish you weren't going back. But I love you, and I'm here for you no matter what." The door stays open. He may need several exits before the final one.

Post-Exit Practical Checklist

When he leaves, there are immediate practical matters to address. This checklist provides a starting point. Not everything will apply to every situation.

Immediate (first week):

- Safe place to stay confirmed
- Basic necessities: clothing, toiletries, medication
- Access to phone (new SIM if she monitors his number)
- Access to money (new bank account if finances were shared or controlled)
- Key documents secured: passport, birth certificate, driver's licence, Medicare card
- GP visit booked (physical health baseline, mental health referral, documentation of stress-related symptoms)

Short-term (first month):

- Legal consultation: family lawyer experienced in high-conflict separation
- Centrelink or financial support options explored if needed
- Therapy or counselling commenced
- Mail redirection organised
- Emergency contacts updated (workplace, medical, school if children involved)
- Digital security reviewed: passwords changed, devices checked for tracking software

Medium-term (first three months):

- Housing situation stabilised
- Custody arrangements formalised if children involved
- Financial separation underway
- Support network identified and engaged
- Return-to-work plan if employment was affected
- Self-care routines established

This list can feel overwhelming. He does not need to do everything immediately. Your role is to help him move through it at a sustainable pace, handling what you can handle, and connecting him with professionals for what requires expertise.

The Money Question

Money will come up. Whether to offer it, how much, under what conditions. This is uncomfortable territory for many families.

Some clarity: Financial support can be the difference between staying and leaving. If he cannot afford a rental bond, cannot pay a lawyer, cannot survive the gap between leaving and financial independence, money is a practical barrier. Removing that barrier may matter more than anything else you do.

If possible, offer without strings. "This is a gift, not a loan. You do not need to pay it back. You do not need to justify how you spend it." Conditional support may reintroduces control into a situation where he has just escaped control. Be clear about what you can actually afford. Do not overextend yourself into financial stress.

Sustainable support matters more than dramatic gestures you cannot maintain. If you cannot offer money, say so simply. "I wish I could help financially. I can't right now. Here's what I can offer instead."

Practical support, time, a spare room, help with job applications. These have value too.

Be cautious about money flowing back to her. In the early weeks, the pull to return is strong. Money given to him may end up funding reconciliation. This is a risk you accept when you give unconditionally. You cannot control what he does with it.

Do not use money as leverage. "I'll help you if you promise not to go back." This positions you as another person trying to control him. He has had enough of that. Consider ongoing versus lump sum. A small regular amount may provide more stability than a large one-off payment.

It also maintains connection: a reason to check in, a recurring reminder that you are there. If siblings or extended family want to contribute, coordinate. A pooled fund with clear communication prevents confusion and resentment.

Money is practical. It is also emotional. It carries weight. Offer it cleanly, without expectation, and let him use it to build whatever comes next.

Positioning for Movement

In Stage Four, "movement" means solidifying the exit into genuine, lasting separation and beginning the work of reconstruction.

Important: This stage is unstable. Apparent progress can reverse quickly. Maintain the patient, non-controlling stance even when things seem to be going well.

- **Create conditions for stability.** Secure housing, consistent routines, and reduced chaos help him build a new foundation from which healing becomes possible.

- **Encourage professional support.** Therapy, support groups, and other professional resources can provide what family cannot. You are too close to be his therapist.

- **Gently support no-contact.** Where possible and safe, reducing contact with her supports recovery. But this is his choice to make and his boundary to set.

- **Be present without smothering.** He needs support but also space. Finding the balance between availability and independence matters.

   Prepare for the long haul. Even a successful exit is followed by months or years of recovery. Stage Four is not the end; it's the beginning of Stage Five.

KEY TAKEAWAY:

- **STAGE FOUR IS FRAGILE.**

- **HE HAS LEFT BUT IS NOT YET STABLE.**

- **EXPECT AMBIVALENCE, GRIEF, AND THE POSSIBILITY OF RETURN.**

- **PROVIDE STABILITY AND PRACTICAL SUPPORT WHILE RESPECTING HIS PACE AND HIS AUTONOMY.**

- **IF HE RETURNS TO HER, KEEP THE DOOR OPEN - MOST VICTIMS LEAVE MULTIPLE TIMES BEFORE LEAVING FOR GOOD.**

Chapter 11: Stage Five - Reconstruction

The exit has stabilised. He is no longer in immediate danger of returning. Now begins the longer, slower work of rebuilding: processing the trauma, rediscovering his identity, and constructing a new life. This stage can take years, and your role continues to evolve.

Recognising This Stage

Stage Five is characterised by stability and forward movement, even though healing is incomplete.

Signs of reconstruction:

- **He is living independently** or in stable housing.

- **Contact with his ex-partner, if any, is managed** and boundaried rather than chaotic.

- **He is processing what happened**: perhaps in therapy, perhaps through his own reflection and developing understanding of the dynamics.

- **He is reconnecting with aspects of himself** that were suppressed: interests, friendships, personality traits.

- **He can talk about the relationship** with more clarity, acknowledging what was harmful rather than defending or minimising.

- **He is beginning to imagine**, and perhaps build, a future that does not include her.

The Dynamic

What She May Be Doing

Her role in his life has diminished, but she may still be present, especially if children are involved.

- **Continued manipulation through children or logistics.** If they share children, she has a permanent channel for influence. Co-parenting can be weaponised: schedule manipulation, undermining his relationship with the children, using exchanges as opportunities for conflict.

- **Periodic hoovering.** Even after the relationship has clearly ended, she may make occasional attempts to reconnect - particularly if she learns he is doing well or is seeing someone new.

- **Moving on herself.** She may enter a new relationship, which can trigger complex feelings in him: relief, jealousy, concern for her new partner.

What He Is Experiencing

- **Ongoing processing.** Understanding what happened takes time. He may have waves of realisation, grief, and anger as he processes different aspects of the abuse. This is not regression; it is the normal pattern of trauma recovery.

- **Identity reformation.** He is rediscovering who he is outside the relationship. This can be exciting and disorienting in equal measure. Preferences, values, and goals that were suppressed are re-emerging; some may have changed.

- **Rebuilding trust.** His capacity to trust others (including you) may be damaged. He may be wary of intimate relationships, suspicious of others' motives, or hesitant to be vulnerable.

- **For men specifically: reconstructing masculine identity.** He must integrate what happened into his sense of himself as a man. This may include confronting cultural messages that taught him to hide distress, minimise harm, or stay silent to preserve pride. Let him redefine strength on his own terms - not as stoicism, but as self-awareness and presence.

What He Needs / What to Avoid

What He Needs

- **Space to become himself again.** The relationship suppressed his authentic self. He needs room to rediscover preferences, interests, and values without pressure to be who he was before or who you wish he were now.

- **Continued acceptance of his pace.** Recovery is not linear. He will have good periods and difficult periods. Continued patience matters, even this far into the journey.

- **A relationship that has evolved.** Your relationship with him is not the same as it was before all this. You have both been through something significant. The relationship that emerges should reflect that: perhaps deeper, perhaps different, but not a simple return to the past.

- **Gentle accountability.** As he heals, he may need to take responsibility for his own patterns, choices, and growth. This is not about blame but about empowerment: recognising his agency in constructing a better future.

What to Avoid

- **Expecting him to be who he was before.** He has been changed by this experience. Some changes may be positive; some may be scars. The person who emerges is not the person who went in, and that is okay.

- **Overprotectiveness.** The instinct to protect him from future hurt is understandable but can become controlling. He needs to make his own choices, including choices that carry risk.

- **Constant references to the past.** While processing is important, he also needs to build a forward-focused identity. If every conversation returns to what happened with her, he cannot fully move on.

You Will Never See Your Old Son Again

This heading may seem harsh, but it contains an important truth. The person who went into this relationship is not the person who came out of it. You will not get that person back, and expecting to will lead to frustration and disappointment.

This is not entirely loss. The person who emerged may, in some ways, be stronger, wiser, more compassionate, more self-aware. Trauma, when processed, can produce growth. The son you have now may have capacities and depths that the son you lost did not.

But some things may be genuinely lost. Innocence. Easy trust. Lightness. Aspects of personality that were worn away by years of suppression. Grieving these losses (yours as well as his) is appropriate.

The task now is to know and love the person he is becoming, rather than mourning the person he was or wishing for someone he cannot be.

Managing the Anger Phase

At some point in recovery (often later than you might expect) anger arrives. The full weight of what was done to him becomes emotionally real, not just intellectually understood. This anger can be intense, consuming, and difficult to live with.

What This Phase Looks Like

He may become preoccupied with what she did, replaying events, recognising manipulation he missed at the time. The rumination phase is where he may want to talk about her constantly, cataloguing her offenses. He may express

rage that feels disproportionate to present circumstances because it contains years of suppressed feeling.

The anger may spill onto others. He may become irritable, short-tempered, or critical. He may express anger at you for not rescuing him sooner, for not being more forceful, for things you said or didn't say during the relationship. This can be painful and confusing when you were on his side all along.

Why This Phase Is Necessary

Anger is a healthy part of recovery. For years, he could not afford to be angry. Anger was dangerous, anger had consequences, anger threatened the carefully maintained equilibrium of the relationship. Now that he is safe, the anger can finally surface.

This anger serves functions: it clarifies that what happened was wrong, it mobilises energy for protection, and it helps him establish that he deserved better. Skipping or suppressing this phase typically means it will return later, often in more destructive forms.

How to Support Through This Phase

- **Let him be angry.** Don't try to rush him past this phase or suggest he should "move on" or "let it go." He needs to feel the anger fully before he can release it.

- **Don't feed the anger excessively.** There's a balance between validating his anger and stoking it. He needs support processing the anger, not a partner in endless rumination about her failings.

- **Set boundaries if anger is directed at you unfairly.** You can accept that he's in a difficult phase without accepting mistreatment. "I understand you're angry, and I'm not going to be spoken to that way" is a reasonable boundary.

- **Encourage professional support.** This is a phase where therapy is particularly valuable. A therapist can help him process the anger without burning out his personal relationships.

- **Trust that it will pass.** The intensity of the anger phase diminishes as it is processed. It may take months, but it will not last forever. The person who emerges on the other side will have integrated this experience in a healthier way.

Trauma Generalisation

As he heals, you may notice patterns that concern you. Responses that seem disproportionate. Suspicion that seems unwarranted. Walls that go up in situations that appear safe. This is trauma generalisation. The lessons his nervous system learned in the abusive relationship have been applied more broadly. His mind is pattern-matching, scanning for threats, and sometimes finding them where they do not exist.

Two common forms:

Blanket mistrust of women.

He was harmed by a woman. His brain has drawn a conclusion: women are dangerous.

This may show up as wariness around female colleagues, reluctance to date, suspicion of women's motives generally. He may make statements that sound bitter or generalising. "Women are all like that." "You can't trust any of them."

This is a protective response, not a permanent belief system. His nervous system is trying to keep him safe by avoiding anything that resembles the source of harm. It will soften as safety is established and as he meets women who do not fit the pattern. Arguing with him about it rarely helps. Gentle exposure to trustworthy women, over time, does.

Stand Again is also designed as a resource that supports genuine healing without sliding into the bitterness that some online spaces cultivate. Communities built on resentment may feel validating initially, but they entrench anger rather than process it. If he is drawn toward red pill or MGTOW content, he is looking for something real: acknowledgment that he was harmed, and a framework that makes sense of it.

Point him toward resources that offer that acknowledgment while also holding space for moving forward. Stand Again at standagain.com.au is one such resource.

Hypersensitivity to narrative.

She constructed narratives about him, about reality, about what was happening. He has learned that stories can be weapons. And he has likely tried to have his voice heard in a society and system not yet ready to hear and believe male victims of family violence. Now he is hypervigilant to anything that feels like narrative that invalidates his experience.

He may react strongly when he hears about domestic violence support for female victims. He may become angry when female victims of domestic violence speak out about their experiences. Or he sees support services being offered to female victims of domestic and family violence.

In his context, this sensitivity makes sense. He lived in a world where the story told about him was a tool of control to dismiss and invalidate his pain. It does not mean he does not sympathise with or believe female victims of domestic violence exits.

His alertness to this narrative is both a survival skill and his pain at the invalidation coming to the surface.

How to Support Through Trauma Generalisation

Give him control over his own story. Do not speak for him. Do not tell others about his experience without his permission. Let him decide what to share and how to frame it. Be transparent. Say what you mean. Avoid spin, softening, or strategic framing, even with good intentions. Directness feels safer than diplomacy. Be patient with the hypervigilance. It will settle as his nervous system learns that safety is real.

In the meantime, he is doing the best he can with a system that was calibrated for threat. Do not take the generalisation personally. If he expresses distrust of women and you are a woman, this is not about you. It is about what happened to him.

Your consistent trustworthiness is the antidote. It just takes time to work.

Stand Again
Support for male victims
of family violence

KEY TAKEAWAY:

- **STAGE FIVE IS ABOUT REBUILDING: IDENTITY, RELATIONSHIPS, AND LIFE.**

- **THE PERSON WHO EMERGES WILL BE DIFFERENT FROM THE PERSON WHO WENT IN – CHANGED BY THE EXPERIENCE, HOPEFULLY GROWN FROM PROCESSING IT.**

- **ACCEPT THAT YOUR OLD SON IS NOT COMING BACK WHILE EMBRACING WHO HE IS BECOMING.**

- **SUPPORT HIM THROUGH THE ANGER PHASE THAT WILL LIKELY ARRIVE, TRUSTING THAT IT IS NECESSARY AND WILL PASS.**

PART FIVE: SAFETY AND THE ABUSER

Chapter 12: Dealing With Her

Your primary relationship is with your son, but his partner is an unavoidable presence in this situation. How you handle contact with her, protect your communications, and navigate safety concerns matters significantly. This chapter provides practical guidance for managing the reality of her existence in your lives.

What to Expect From Her

Understanding her likely behaviours helps you prepare for what's coming and avoid being caught off guard. While every abuser is different, certain patterns are common enough to anticipate.

For families supporting a man, it is important to recognise that many of these behaviours are interpreted differently when the victim is male. Her charm is more believable. Her distress is taken more seriously. His discomfort is often dismissed as moodiness or poor communication skills. These biases shape how outsiders interpret the dynamic, which is why her public face is so effective.

The Public Face

Many abusers maintain a carefully constructed public persona that bears little resemblance to their private behaviour. She may appear charming, warm, and reasonable in social settings. She may seem devoted to your son, attentive to his needs, and confused about why anyone would have concerns.

This discrepancy between public and private faces can be disorienting. You may find yourself wondering if you've imagined the problem, if perhaps you've misunderstood, if the person you're seeing at family gatherings is the "real" her. She is counting on this confusion.

The public face serves multiple purposes: it provides plausible deniability, it recruits allies who see only the charming version, and it makes your son's

complaints seem unreasonable if he ever voices them. "She seems so nice - surely it can't be that bad."

Charm Offensives

She may actively try to win you over, particularly early in the relationship or when she senses your concern. This might include gifts, expressions of appreciation for your family, efforts to include herself in family traditions, or confidential conversations where she positions herself as your ally in helping your son.

These charm offensives can be confusing. Part of you may want to believe the nice version is real. And in some cases, she may genuinely want connection with his family. Abusers are complex people, not cartoon villains, and their desire for acceptance can be real even alongside their harmful behaviour.

The problem is that charm does not equal safety. This charm often lands even more strongly when the victim is male because culturally we are conditioned to see men as resilient and women as relationally vulnerable. A charming, agreeable woman fits the social script; a man who reports being controlled does not. She knows this, and she uses it.

However pleasant she is to you, the dynamics of the relationship with your son remain what they are. Being charmed into complacency serves her purposes; it does not serve his.

Information Gathering

She may use interactions with you to gather information: about your family, about your concerns, about what your son has told you. Conversations that seem casual may have strategic purposes. Questions about family finances, health, or conflicts can provide material for later use.

She may also gather information by monitoring his communications with you. Text messages, emails, and phone calls may not be private. Assume anything you communicate might reach her unless you have taken specific steps to secure it.

Triangulation

Triangulation involves using third parties to manage relationships indirectly. She may communicate with you in ways designed to create conflict between you and your son, or between different family members.

This might look like telling you things your son supposedly said (which may be distorted or invented), sharing "concerns" about his behaviour that position her as the reasonable one, or expressing hurt about how his family treats her in ways designed to make him defend her against you.

When you find yourself in conflict with your son or other family members over something she reported, triangulation may be at work.

Also, when the victim is male, triangulation is especially effective because outsiders instinctively trust her emotional expressions more than his restraint. His calmness becomes misread as indifference; her tears become misread as truth.

Escalation When Threatened

If she perceives threat to her control (whether from your family's involvement, his growing awareness, or actual movement toward separation) expect escalation. The specific form depends on her patterns, but common escalations include:

- Increased restrictions on his contact with family
- Manufactured crises that demand his attention and energy
- Intensified criticism and control within the relationship
- Threats to herself, to him, to the children, to his reputation
- Direct attacks on family members she perceives as threats
- Pregnancy or other major commitments that increase his entanglement

Understanding that escalation is likely when the status quo is threatened helps you plan accordingly and avoid actions that predictably trigger it without compensating benefit.

Families also often underestimate escalation because men rarely admit fear. But fear is present - he just masks it. This is why even mild increases in suspicion or tension from her side can destabilise him.

Social Media and the Public Narrative

You scroll through your phone and there it is: a photo of them at a restaurant, smiling. Her caption talks about "date night with my love" and "so grateful for this man." The comments are full of heart emojis and "you two are so cute!"

You know what their life actually looks like. And yet here is the performance of happiness, broadcast to everyone.

The Performed Relationship

Social media is curated reality. Everyone presents a polished version of their life. But in coercive control relationships, this performance serves specific functions:

- **It provides cover.** If anyone suspects something is wrong, the public narrative contradicts it. "They always look so happy on Instagram." The performance becomes evidence against the abuse.

- **It creates witnesses.** Friends and acquaintances who see the public happiness become implicit supporters of the relationship. They form the audience she can later recruit if the relationship is challenged.

- **It traps him further.** The more public the performance of happiness, the more humiliating it would be to admit the reality. He has participated in constructing this image; dismantling it feels like admitting he has been lying.

- **It rewrites history.** The social media record becomes a kind of evidence of the relationship they supposedly had, of how they supposedly treated each other. It's hard to claim abuse when the photographic record shows smiles.

Managing Your Exposure

Seeing the performance is painful. You know the reality; the performance feels like gaslighting directed at you.

- **Limit your exposure.** You can mute, unfollow, or hide their content without unfriending. You don't need to see every post. Checking compulsively hurts you and helps no one.

- **Remember what you know.** The photos are not reality. The captions are not truth. Your knowledge of the situation is not invalidated by a curated feed.

- **Resist the urge to comment.** Leaving comments that hint at the truth, subtweet, or undermine the performance - this is tempting but counterproductive. It provides evidence of your hostility and likely triggers consequences for him.

When She Controls the Story

She may use social media to shape broader narrative. Not just about the relationship but about you. Vague posts about "toxic people" or "setting boundaries with family." Comments that position her as the victim of your interference.

This public narrative-building can feel intolerable. You want to defend yourself, correct the record, tell the truth.

- **Don't fight the narrative publicly.** Social media arguments never look good for anyone. Responding to her posts gives them oxygen and makes you look reactive.

- **Speak privately to people who matter.** If close friends or family see her posts and ask, you can share your perspective one-on-one. But avoid broad campaigns to tell "your side" This creates drama that serves no one.

- **Trust that behaviour reveals itself.** People who know you will weigh her online narrative against their actual experience of you. Over time, character shows through in ways that curated posts cannot obscure.

When He Participates in the Performance

He may be posting too: his own tributes to her, photos of their "perfect" life, captions that seem to come from a stranger.

This is part of the adapted self. He may be performing for her approval, demonstrating loyalty, or simply doing what is required to maintain peace. The posts may be genuine expressions of his current reality - a reality shaped by her framework.

Don't confront him about the disconnect between his posts and what you know. This puts him in an impossible position and likely triggers defensiveness.

When he eventually emerges from the relationship, the social media record may be painful for him to see - evidence of how fully he participated in the constructed reality. He will process this in his own time.

How to Handle Contact With Her

You are dealing with someone skilled at shaping narratives, exploiting social biases, and manipulating emotional responses - especially when the victim is male

Your goal in contact with her is therefore simple: don't make things worse.

You are not going to change her, convince her, or win against her in direct confrontation. Your focus is protecting your relationship with your son and avoiding actions that give her ammunition.

The Grey Rock Method

The grey rock method involves making yourself as uninteresting and unreactive as possible. Like a grey rock, you offer nothing to grab onto: no drama, no emotional reactions, no engaging content.

In practice, this means keeping interactions brief and neutral. Answer questions with minimal information. Don't volunteer details about your life, your feelings, or your concerns. Don't rise to provocations or take bait. Be polite but boring.

Grey rock is not about being cold or hostile. That gives her something to work with. It's about being pleasant but uninformative, engaged but not engaging. "That's nice." "I see." "We'll have to think about that." Responses that acknowledge without extending.

With male victims, even neutrality can be spun into hostility. This is why "pleasant neutrality" is essential. Anything sharper becomes ammunition she uses to reinforce her story that "his family hates me."

At Family Gatherings

When she attends family events, your job is to be cordial without being intimate. Include her as you would any guest, but don't attempt to build a special relationship or have significant private conversations.

Avoid creating situations where she might feel excluded or targeted. This gives her legitimate grievance and provides material for later use with your son. Treat her with the polite neutrality you would extend to anyone.

If she attempts to draw you into private conversation, keep it brief. If she raises concerns about your son or the relationship, don't engage substantively. "I appreciate you sharing that. I'm sure you two will work it out."

When She Seeks Alliance

She may attempt to position herself as your ally. Sharing concerns about your son, confiding difficulties, seeking your support in managing him. This can feel flattering and may even contain elements of genuine connection.

Be cautious. Information you share may be used against you or your son. Agreements you make may be reported to him in distorted form. The alliance she's offering likely serves her purposes more than yours.

You can acknowledge her communications without engaging deeply. "I can see things are stressful. I hope you two can work through it." This is not a rejection, but it's also not an alliance.

When She Attacks

She may directly attack you - accusing you of undermining the relationship, criticising your parenting, blaming you for problems. These attacks may come directly or through your son.

Do not counter-attack. This is what she may be hoping for. Attacks from her often land socially because people default to believing the woman in heterosexual conflict.

She may be looking for evidence of your hostility that can be shown to your son. Your restraint protects your credibility and later, his. Respond minimally: "I'm sorry you feel that way." "That's not my intention." "I hope we can move past this."

If attacks come through your son, avoid putting him in the middle. "I hear that she's upset. I'm not going to argue about this with you. I love you, and I'm here for you."

If You Must Communicate With Her

Sometimes direct communication is unavoidable. Logistics around events, issues involving grandchildren, or situations where she has initiated contact that requires response.

Keep It Written When Possible

Text or email creates a record. Phone calls and in-person conversations can be reported inaccurately; written communication speaks for itself. When you need to communicate, prefer formats that document what was actually said.

Keep your written communications brief, factual, and neutral in tone. Avoid anything that could be taken out of context or read as hostile. Before sending, ask yourself how this message would look if shown to others - because it just may be.

The BIFF Method

BIFF stands for Brief, Informative, Friendly, and Firm. This framework is useful for written communication with high-conflict individuals:

- **Brief**: Keep it short. Long messages provide more material to argue with or misinterpret. Say what needs to be said and stop.
- **Informative**: Stick to facts and logistics. Avoid emotional content, opinions, or anything that invites debate.
- **Friendly**: Maintain a pleasant tone. This is not about being fake; it's about not giving ammunition. A friendly message is harder to frame as hostile.
- **Firm**: End the conversation. Don't leave openings for extended back-and-forth. "Let me know if that works" is better than "What do you think about..."

Don't JADE

JADE stands for Justify, Argue, Defend, Explain. With high-conflict individuals, these responses tend to extend conflict rather than resolve it.

When she challenges or criticises, resist the urge to justify your actions, argue your position, defend yourself, or explain your reasoning. These responses invite counter-responses, and the conflict escalates.

Instead, acknowledge and redirect. "I understand you see it differently. Here's what we're able to do..." You haven't conceded, but you haven't engaged in a battle you cannot win.

Digital Security

In coercive control relationships, abusers often monitor their partner's communications. Assume that your son's phone, email, and social media may not be private. Planning your communication accordingly protects both of you.

Assume Monitoring

She may have access to his devices through shared passwords, spyware, or simply by checking his phone when he's not looking. She may monitor his social media, his email, his text messages.

For routine communication, this may not matter. There is nothing wrong with a parent texting their son about dinner plans. But if you need to communicate something sensitive - if he's reaching out for help, if you're discussing his situation - assume she may see it.

This assumption should shape what you write. Don't put anything in a text or email that would be dangerous if she read it.

Creating Secure Channels

If secure communication becomes necessary, particularly if he's moving toward exit, there are ways to create channels she's less likely to access:

- **Secondary devices.** A cheap prepaid phone that he keeps hidden can provide a communication channel she doesn't know about. This is useful if he's planning departure and needs to coordinate logistics.

- **Encrypted messaging.** Apps with end-to-end encryption provide more security than standard texting. However, if she has access to his phone, she can still read messages on the device itself.

- **Disappearing messages.** Some apps offer messages that delete after being read. This prevents her from finding a history of sensitive conversations.

- **In-person communication.** When possible, sensitive conversations happen in person, away from devices that might be monitored.

The level of security needed depends on the situation. For most of the journey, routine communication is fine. As things escalate toward potential exit, secure channels become more important.

Protecting Your Own Information

Consider what information about you is accessible and whether it matters. Your address, workplace, daily schedule, financial situation: could any of this be used against you or your son?

In most cases, you don't need to go to extreme measures. But if the situation involves threats or potential for escalation beyond normal conflict, basic digital hygiene matters: strong passwords, limited social media exposure, awareness of what's publicly accessible about you.

When to Consider Involving Authorities

Involving police, courts, or other authorities is a significant step with unpredictable consequences. It should not be undertaken lightly - but there are situations where it becomes necessary.

The Reality for Male Victims

Before discussing when to involve authorities, it's important to acknowledge the particular challenges male victims face. When police respond to domestic violence calls, they may assume the man is the perpetrator. When courts hear abuse allegations, they may give more credibility to the woman's account.

Your son may have legitimate fears about involving authorities: fear of being arrested himself, fear of not being believed, fear of losing custody of children. These fears are not paranoid; they reflect documented patterns in how systems respond to male victims.

This doesn't mean authorities should never be involved. It means involvement should be strategic, documented, and ideally guided by professionals who understand these dynamics.

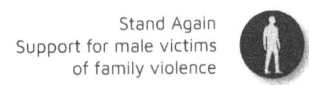

Clear Triggers for Involvement

Certain situations warrant immediate involvement of authorities regardless of complications:

- **Immediate physical danger.** If someone is being physically harmed or there's imminent threat of physical harm, call emergency services.

- **Children at risk.** If children are being abused or neglected, child protection obligations apply regardless of other considerations.

- **Credible threats.** If she has made specific, credible threats of violence against him, against herself, against others - these should be reported and documented.

- **Criminal behaviour.** If she has committed crimes: assault, theft, fraud, property destruction - reporting creates documentation even if prosecution doesn't follow.

Strategic Considerations

Outside of immediate safety situations, involving authorities is a strategic decision with potential benefits and costs:

- **Documentation value.** Police reports and court records create official documentation that may be valuable later - in custody disputes, in establishing patterns, in protecting against false accusations.

- **Escalation risk.** Involving authorities often escalates conflict. She may retaliate with her own allegations. The situation may become more dangerous rather than safer.

- **His readiness.** If he's not ready to engage with authorities himself, your involvement may complicate his situation or damage your relationship with him.

When possible, decisions about involving authorities should be made with professional guidance: a domestic violence advocate, a lawyer familiar with these dynamics, or other experts who can help assess the specific situation.

Safety Planning

Safety planning means thinking through potential risks and how to address them before they become crises. The level of safety planning needed depends on the specific situation. Some relationships involve little physical danger; others involve significant risk.

Assessing Risk

Risk factors that warrant more intensive safety planning include:

- History of physical violence in the relationship
- Access to weapons
- History of threats, particularly specific threats about what happens if he leaves
- Mental health issues including personality disorders or substance abuse
- Escalating intensity of control or abuse
- Statements suggesting she would rather destroy things than lose control
- Isolation from all support systems except her

The period when he is leaving or has just left is statistically the most dangerous time.

And for male victims, safety planning is complicated by social disbelief. If he anticipates not being believed by police or service providers, he may minimise danger. Families often need to compensate for this by taking threats more seriously than he feels permitted to.

Safety planning therefore should intensify as exit approaches.

Elements of a Safety Plan

A safety plan addresses practical questions about how to stay safe during and after exit:

- **Safe location.** Where will he go that she cannot easily access? Your home may be obvious; are there alternatives? Does the location need to be kept confidential?

- **Important documents.** Passport, birth certificate, financial documents, and other important papers should be secured or copied before exit if possible.

- **Financial access.** Does he have access to money she cannot control? If finances are shared or she controls them, how will he manage immediate expenses?

- **Children's safety.** If children are involved, how will their safety and care be managed? What are the custody implications of various exit scenarios?

- **Communication plan.** How will he communicate safely? Who needs to know what, and when?

- **Emergency contacts.** Who should be contacted in various emergency scenarios? What information do they need in advance?

- **Legal preparation.** Has he consulted with a lawyer about protective orders, custody, divorce proceedings? Is documentation in place?

Your Role in Safety Planning

Your role depends on his stage and readiness. In early stages, safety planning may be something you think about privately, preparing what you can offer when the time comes. In later stages, you may actively participate in developing and executing a plan.

Key contributions you can make:

- **Providing safe space.** Your home may be part of his safety plan. Is it secure? Is the location known to her? Can you accommodate him (and possibly children) for an extended period?

- **Financial resources.** Can you provide emergency funds? Can you help with deposits, legal fees, or other costs of separation?

- **Holding documents.** Important documents stored at your location are safer than documents in a home she can access.

- **Being a communication hub.** Coordinating communication among family members who are supporting his exit.

- **Connecting with professionals.** Identifying lawyers, therapists, domestic violence services, and other professionals before they're urgently needed.

Professional Resources

For high-risk situations, professional help with safety planning is valuable. Domestic violence services - though often oriented toward female victims - can provide expertise. Some organisations specifically serve male victims. Lawyers with domestic violence experience can advise on legal protections.

Globally, Stand Again (www.standagain.com.au) provides coaching support for men affected by family violence, including safety planning assistance.

For immediate danger situations, emergency services in Australia (000) should always be the first call.

KEY TAKEAWAY:

- MANAGING THE ABUSER REQUIRES STRATEGIC PATIENCE:

- EXPECT CHARM AND MANIPULATION, HANDLE CONTACT WITH GREY ROCK NEUTRALITY, COMMUNICATE USING BIFF PRINCIPLES, AND ASSUME YOUR COMMUNICATIONS MAY BE MONITORED.

- INVOLVING AUTHORITIES IS COMPLICATED FOR MALE VICTIMS AND SHOULD BE CAREFULLY CONSIDERED.

- SAFETY PLANNING BECOMES CRITICAL AS EXIT APPROACHES - KNOW THE RISKS, PREPARE RESOURCES, AND CONNECT WITH PROFESSIONALS WHO CAN HELP NAVIGATE HIGH-RISK SITUATIONS.

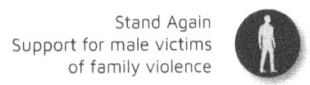

PART SIX: SPECIFIC COMPLICATIONS

Chapter 13: Complications

Every situation has its own complexity. This chapter addresses specific circumstances that may apply to your son's situation, each of which adds layers to an already difficult dynamic. Not all sections will be relevant to you: read what applies and skip what doesn't.

When Children Are Involved

Children change everything. They create permanent ties that cannot be severed by separation. They become leverage in ways that adults alone cannot be leveraged. And they face their own risks in an abusive household that your son may be staying specifically to mitigate.

Why He Stays for the Children

Your son may believe that staying in the relationship is the best way to protect his children. His calculations might include:

- **Presence as protection.** While he's there, he can buffer the children from her behaviour. He can provide stability, model healthy responses, and intervene when things escalate. If he leaves, the children may face her alone.

- **Custody fears.** Family courts often favour mothers, particularly in Australia. He may fear that leaving means losing meaningful access to his children - seeing them every other weekend rather than every day. The statistics for fathers' custody outcomes support this fear.

- **False accusation risk.** In custody disputes, false allegations of abuse by the father are not uncommon. He may fear that leaving triggers accusations that result in supervised visitation or loss of access entirely – even if later proven false.

- **Children as hostages.** She may have made clear, explicitly or implicitly, what happens to his relationship with the children if he leaves. They function as hostages to his compliance.

For men, these fears are often reinforced by what they have seen happen to other fathers: reduced time, supervised contact on thin evidence, or systems that treat any concern he raises as potential aggression.

He is not only fighting his partner's control; he is also bracing for a system that may assume he is the problem before it has heard a word from him.

These calculations are not irrational. They may even be correct. The decision to stay for the children, while painful to watch, may reflect genuine assessment of impossible options.

The Impact on Children

Children in homes with coercive control are affected even when they are not directly targeted. They absorb the atmosphere of tension. They learn distorted models of relationships. They may be triangulated, manipulated, or used as pawns.

Your grandchildren may exhibit signs of distress: anxiety, behavioural problems, difficulty at school, withdrawal, or precocious caretaking behaviours. They may seem unusually attuned to adult moods, or they may have learned to suppress their own needs.

You may feel urgency to protect them, to report to child services, to intervene directly, to rescue them from the situation. These impulses are understandable but require careful consideration. Interventions that fail can make things worse for everyone, including the children.

Your Role with the Grandchildren

- **Be a stable presence.** Your relationship with your grandchildren matters. Time with you provides them with an alternative model. A home where relationships work differently, where they can relax, where they are loved without conditions.

- **Don't put them in the middle.** Avoid questioning them about what happens at home, using them to send messages, or making them feel responsible for the adult situation. They are already carrying too much.

- **Watch for serious harm.** If you observe evidence of direct abuse or neglect of the children. Not just the general dysfunction of the household - you may have legal obligations to report. Consult with professionals before making this decision, as reports that don't result in action can make access to the children more difficult.

- **Support their relationship with their father.** Whatever happens with the adult relationship, help the children maintain connection with your son. They need him, and he needs them. When systems or others minimise his importance, your steady affirmation that he is a safe, loving parent counteracts a powerful cultural story that often sidelines fathers.

After Separation

If he does leave, children become the ongoing battleground. Co-parenting with an abuser is extraordinarily difficult. She may use custody arrangements to maintain control, manipulate the children's perceptions of their father, or create conflict at every exchange.

Your son may need support navigating the family court system, which is often poorly equipped to recognise coercive control dynamics. Legal advice from lawyers experienced in high-conflict custody matters is valuable.

Your continued relationship with the grandchildren during and after separation may require navigating her gatekeeping. Stay committed to maintaining that relationship: it matters to them and to you.

Pregnancy or New Baby

Learning that your son's partner is pregnant or has recently had a baby creates particular anguish. The entanglement deepens permanently. The timeline for any resolution extends. And yet a child is coming who will be your grandchild, whatever the circumstances.

Pregnancy as Tactic

In some abusive relationships, pregnancy is strategic. A baby creates permanent connection, increases his practical and emotional entanglement, and makes leaving vastly more complicated. The timing of pregnancy (particularly if it coincides with moments when he seemed to be pulling away) may not be coincidental.

This does not mean the pregnancy is not also wanted or loved. Motivations are complex. But recognising that pregnancy serves strategic purposes helps explain why it happens when it does.

Your Response to the News

When he tells you she is pregnant, your response matters. Whatever you are feeling (and your feelings will be complicated) he needs you to respond to the baby as a grandchild, not as a trap.

Expressing appropriate congratulations does not mean abandoning your concerns. It means recognising that this child will exist regardless of your feelings, and that your relationship with both your son and the child depends on how you navigate this moment.

Later, in private, you can process your grief about what this means for the situation. But in the moment of announcement, be a parent welcoming news of a grandchild.

During Pregnancy and Early Parenthood

Pregnancy and new parenthood are vulnerable times. Abuse often escalates during pregnancy, when she may feel more secure in his commitment or when his attention to the baby triggers her insecurity.

Stay connected. Offer practical support, help with preparations, presence during the chaos of early parenthood. Your involvement provides both support and witness. It keeps the door open during a time when he may feel especially trapped.

Be prepared for her to gatekeep access to the baby. Some abusers restrict grandparent involvement as another form of control. Navigate this as gracefully as you can, prioritising maintaining whatever access you have.

Addiction

When addiction: alcohol, drugs, gambling, or other compulsive behaviours is present alongside coercive control, the situation becomes significantly more complex. The addictive behaviour may belong to him, to her, or to both.

His Addiction

If your son has developed addictive patterns, these may be responses to the stress of his situation. Ways of coping with the constant tension, numbing himself to what his life has become. Addiction that develops or worsens within the relationship may be a symptom as much as a separate problem.

His addiction may also be used against him. She may threaten to expose his addiction in custody disputes or to his employer. For a man, this leverage is particularly potent because it feeds existing stereotypes: the unreliable father, the dangerous partner, the man who cannot be trusted. She does not need the full story; she only needs enough truth to make the worst version of him sound plausible.

She may even enable the addiction while also using it as evidence of his failures.

Addressing addiction while still in a coercive control relationship is extremely difficult. The conditions that fuel the addiction are still present. Recovery typically requires leaving the relationship, but the addiction may make leaving harder by affecting his judgment, depleting his resources, and providing her with ammunition.

Her Addiction

If she has addiction issues, this adds volatility and unpredictability to an already unstable situation. Her behaviour may be more erratic. The household may be more chaotic. His caretaking role may extend to managing her addiction, creating additional ties that feel impossible to sever.

He may stay partly because he fears what happens to her if he leaves. His protective instincts, already exploited by the relationship, are amplified by her apparent vulnerability. Leaving someone with an addiction can feel like abandonment, even when staying is destroying him.

Navigating Dual Issues

When both addiction and coercive control are present, treatment becomes complicated. Addiction services may not recognise or address the coercive control. Domestic violence services may not be equipped for addiction issues. Finding professionals who can hold both realities is valuable but not easy.

Your approach should address both without conflating them. Addiction does not excuse abuse - his or hers. Coercive control does not excuse addiction. Both need to be addressed, ideally with professional help that understands the interaction.

Financial Dependence

Financial abuse is a common component of coercive control, and financial dependence (whether his on her or hers on him) creates practical barriers to exit that compound the psychological ones.

When He Is Financially Dependent

If she controls the finances, he may have limited access to money, no independent savings, and no clear path to supporting himself after exit. He may not have his own bank account, or she may monitor it closely. Large purchases or withdrawals may require her approval.

Financial dependence created during the relationship (whether through her insistence that he not work, through depleting his savings, or through debt accumulated in his name) creates practical imprisonment. He cannot leave because he literally cannot afford to.

Your role may include providing financial resources for exit: money for deposits, legal fees, living expenses until he can stabilise. This is a significant commitment that should be made carefully, but financial support can be the practical difference between being trapped and being free.

When She Is Financially Dependent

If he is the primary earner and she does not work or earns significantly less, he may feel responsible for her welfare even as she harms him. Leaving means leaving her without financial support. His sense of duty as a provider (a core masculine identity for many men) can make this feel impossible.

He may also fear the financial consequences of separation: spousal support obligations, division of assets that depletes his resources, the cost of maintaining two households. The financial devastation of divorce may seem worse than the ongoing devastation of the marriage.

For many men, this fear is tangled up with identity: the protector, the provider, the man who does not "abandon" someone who relies on him financially. She knows this, and she leans hard on that narrative whenever he contemplates leaving.

Understanding the actual financial and legal realities, rather than the fears, requires consultation with a family lawyer. The picture may not be as catastrophic as he fears, or there may be ways to structure exit that minimise damage.

When His Therapist Doesn't See It

Professional help should support recognition and recovery. But therapists are not uniformly trained in coercive control dynamics, and some may inadvertently reinforce the patterns that are harming him.

This problem is magnified when the victim is male. **Many clinicians have never been trained to imagine a man as the primary victim in a**

heterosexual relationship. Without realising it, they may interpret his confusion as emotional immaturity and her distress as evidence.

How Therapy Can Go Wrong

- **Couples therapy with an abuser.** Couples therapy assumes two partners working in good faith toward improvement. With an abuser, it becomes another venue for manipulation. She may use sessions to gather information, present her version of reality to a professional, or frame him as the problem. Couples therapy is generally contraindicated where coercive control is present.

- **Therapists who don't recognise abuse.** A therapist without training in coercive control towards male victims may hear about relationship difficulties and apply standard relationship advice: communicate more, take responsibility for your part, work on meeting her needs. This advice, appropriate in healthy relationships, can be harmful in abusive ones - reinforcing his self-blame and her framework.

- **Therapists who have been co-opted.** Some abusers successfully charm therapists, presenting as the reasonable, long-suffering partner. The therapist may begin to see your son through her framework, subtly reinforcing her narrative about his failures.

- **Gender assumptions.** Therapists, like everyone else, carry assumptions about domestic abuse. The assumption that men are perpetrators and women are victims can blind professionals to what is actually happening when the genders are reversed.

Your son may feel that therapy is another place where he must defend himself rather than be understood. If he has had this experience once, it can make him wary of seeking help again.

What You Can Do

You cannot control his therapeutic relationship, and directly criticising his therapist is likely to backfire. But you can:

- Ask gentle questions about how therapy is going, listening for signs that it's helping or harming.

- If he expresses doubts about his therapist, support him in considering alternatives.

- Be aware that couples therapy in this situation may be making things worse, even if it sounds like a positive step.

- If he's seeking individual therapy, gently suggest looking for someone with experience in trauma or domestic violence.

- Where possible, encourage him to choose someone who explicitly acknowledges working with male victims. Seeing those words on a website or profile can reduce the shame he feels and increase the likelihood that he will be believed.

- When he does exit, help him find appropriate therapeutic support. Someone who understands coercive control and can support his recovery rather than reinforcing his self-blame.

Religious or Cultural Dimensions

Religious beliefs and cultural backgrounds can add layers of complexity, creating additional pressure to stay or shaping how the situation is understood by everyone involved.

Religious Barriers to Leaving

Many religious traditions emphasise the permanence of marriage and the sinfulness of divorce. If your son is religious, he may feel that leaving violates his faith, that divorce is not an option regardless of circumstances, or that his suffering is a test to be endured.

Religious communities may reinforce these beliefs, pressuring him to stay, to forgive, to try harder. Religious leaders without training in abuse dynamics may offer counsel that sounds spiritual but is practically harmful: pray more, submit more, love more sacrificially.

For a man, this often lands as a demand to endure silently. His suffering becomes framed as noble, his reluctance to leave becomes proof of faithfulness, and any thought of protecting himself feels like spiritual failure.

His partner may weaponise religious beliefs: using his faith to enforce compliance, framing her demands as aligned with God's will, or threatening spiritual consequences for leaving.

Cultural Expectations

Cultural backgrounds shape expectations about marriage, gender roles, family honour, and acceptable responses to relationship difficulties. Some cultures emphasise family cohesion so strongly that individual suffering is minimised. Some have strict gender expectations that make male victimhood especially shameful. In such environments, admitting that a woman is harming him may feel like confessing to being less of a man. The shame of disclosure can feel heavier than the pain of staying.

Extended family and community may apply pressure based on the cultural values. Divorce may bring shame on the family. Admitting to being controlled by a woman may be unthinkable within his cultural context.

If your family comes from a cultural background with strong expectations around marriage and family, these pressures may be affecting your son in ways that add to the barriers he faces.

Navigating Religious and Cultural Factors

Religious and cultural dimensions require respect, even when they seem to be keeping him trapped. These are not simply obstacles to be overcome but core aspects of his identity that he needs to integrate with his situation.

Some approaches that may help:

- Finding religious resources that address abuse. Most major faiths have teachings that do not require victims to remain in abusive situations, though these may not be the teachings he has encountered.

- Identifying religious leaders or community members who understand abuse dynamics and can offer counsel that is both spiritually grounded and practically sound.

- Respecting his need to find a path forward that is consistent with his values, even if that path is different from what you would choose.

- Examining your own family's cultural messages about marriage, divorce, and help-seeking to ensure you are not adding to the pressure.

When You Discover He's Been Aggressive

You may learn from him, from her, or from others that your son has behaved aggressively in the relationship. This information is confusing and painful. It may make you question whether you've understood the situation correctly.

Understanding Reactive Abuse

Victims of sustained abuse sometimes react in ways that are themselves abusive. After months or years of psychological torment, he may snap: yelling, throwing things, shoving, or striking. This reactive abuse does not make him the abuser, but it does make the situation more complicated.

Reactive abuse is often exactly what the abuser has been working toward. By provoking a reaction, she obtains evidence that he is the dangerous one. She can now claim victimhood, point to his behaviour as the real problem, and use his reaction to control the narrative with family, friends, and potentially courts.

If your son has reacted aggressively, he may be filled with shame. He may feel he has proven her right about him. He may have provided her with leverage she will use against him. The aggressive reaction, whatever its context, is now part of the record.

When the victim is male, this single incident often becomes the entire story in the eyes of outsiders. Police, courts, therapists, and even extended family may fixate on his reaction while ignoring the years of provocation that led to it.

Distinguishing Patterns

One aggressive incident by a person who has been relentlessly tormented is different from a pattern of using aggression to control. The questions that matter are about patterns, not isolated incidents:

- **Who is generally afraid of whom?** In coercive control relationships, fear flows primarily in one direction.

- **Who is modifying their behaviour to avoid the other's reactions?** The victim walks carefully; the abuser does not.

- **Who has more freedom in the relationship?** The person who can come and go as they please is not the primary victim.

- **What is the history?** A single explosive reaction after years of control is different from a pattern of using aggression to dominate.

None of this excuses aggressive behaviour. But understanding context matters for understanding what is happening and how to help.

Supporting Him Without Excusing Harm

If your son has been aggressive, he needs to take responsibility for that behaviour. Supporting him doesn't mean pretending it didn't happen or that it was acceptable.

What it does mean is helping him understand the context without using context as excuse. He can simultaneously recognise that he was provoked and that his reaction was wrong. He can understand that her behaviour created the conditions while still owning his response.

Therapeutic support is especially important here. He needs to process what happened, understand the dynamics that led to it, develop better coping strategies, and genuinely reckon with any harm he caused. This work is difficult but essential.

Work as an Anchor Point

His job may be one of the few areas of his life she does not fully control. Work can function as an anchor point. A place where he maintains identity, relationships, and competence outside her influence.

Work as Refuge

For many men in coercive control relationships, work is the one place they still feel competent and valued. While home is a minefield of unpredictable expectations and constant failure, work offers clear tasks, achievable goals, and recognition for performance.

This is why some men in abusive relationships throw themselves into work. Not just as escape but as identity maintenance. At work, they can still be the person they understand themselves to be. The long hours that may look like workaholism may be reluctance to return to an environment where nothing they do is ever enough.

For many men, competence at work is the last surviving piece of their self-respect. When everything at home tells him he is useless, stupid, or broken, a functioning career is proof to himself that this story is not entirely true.

Work relationships can also be significant. Colleagues may provide social contact that has been otherwise eliminated. A trusted coworker may be someone he can talk to. The workplace offers a community outside her control.

When She Targets His Work

Recognising work as a refuge, she may target it. This might include:

- Creating crises that require him to miss work or leave early
- Calling or texting constantly during work hours, demanding immediate responses
- Showing up at his workplace unexpectedly
- Creating conflict with his work schedule: appointments, demands, or expectations that conflict with professional obligations
- Sabotaging his work performance through sleep deprivation, manufactured stress, or other interference
- Criticising his work relationships, particularly with female colleagues

If his work performance is suffering, or if he has lost jobs during the relationship, these patterns may be at play.

Job loss or underperformance is then used as further "evidence" that he is inadequate. The very thing that once anchored his identity becomes another stick to beat him with.

Supporting the Work Anchor

Encourage him to protect his work. Not because career is more important than relationship, but because work may be the last sphere where he maintains independence, competence, and outside relationships.

If he has trusted relationships at work, these may be significant. Without prying, you can express general support for his professional relationships and achievements. When he talks about work, engage with genuine interest, this is a part of his life that may still feel like his.

When He's Left and Returned Before

If your son has previously left the relationship and then returned, you know the particular heartbreak of watching the door close again after it seemed to be opening. Multiple departures and returns are common in abusive relationships and understanding this pattern helps you respond effectively.

Why People Return

Research suggests victims of abuse often leave multiple times before leaving permanently. Returns happen for many reasons:

- **The trauma bond.** The neurological attachment created by intermittent reinforcement does not dissolve because he has physically left. He misses her. He loves her. The withdrawal is painful enough that returning seems like relief.

- **Her promises.** She promises to change. She seems genuinely remorseful. The person he fell in love with reappears, and he wants to believe that person is the real her.

- **Practical difficulties.** The chaos of exit: housing, finances, logistics may seem more overwhelming than the familiar patterns of the relationship. The devil he knows feels safer than the chaos he doesn't.

- **Pressure from others.** Well-meaning people may encourage reconciliation. Religious or cultural pressure may be applied. Mutual friends may tell him he's overreacting.

- **The children.** If children are involved, he may return to be with them daily rather than see them according to a custody schedule.

- **Incomplete processing.** If he left during crisis without having fully worked through what was happening, he may not yet have the framework to understand why return is dangerous.

After a Return

When he returns to her after leaving, your response matters:

- **Don't punish him.** The temptation to withdraw, to express disgust, to refuse contact is understandable. But punishment closes doors you need to keep open. He will need you again.

- **Express concern without ultimatums.** "I'm worried about you. I wish you weren't going back. But I love you, and I'm here for you." Say this once, clearly, and then stop repeating it.

- **Maintain connection.** The principles from earlier in this book apply. Return to leaving the light on. Maintain warm contact without constant pressure.

- **Prepare for next time.** Each departure, even when followed by return, may be part of a process. What you learned about helping him during the last exit will be useful when the next exit comes.

Multiple Cycles

If this pattern has repeated multiple times, managing your own emotional response becomes essential. Each cycle is devastating: the hope of departure followed by the grief of return. You may feel yourself becoming cynical, withdrawn, or burnt out.

This is where your support system matters. Process your own feelings outside the relationship with him. Maintain sustainable hope: hope that holds open possibility without attaching to any timeline. Each departure, even if followed by return, may be building toward the departure that sticks.

Some people do stay permanently. That possibility is real and must be accommodated, even while maintaining hope for eventual exit. Part Eight of this book addresses what it means if he never leaves.

> **Key Takeaway:**
>
> - **Every situation has specific complications that add layers to an already difficult dynamic.**
>
> - **Whether children, pregnancy, addiction, finances, unhelpful therapy, religious pressure, his own reactive behaviour, his work, or previous failed exits – these factors shape what is possible and what you can offer.**
>
> - **Understanding the specific complications of your situation helps you respond more effectively while maintaining the core**
>
> - **principles of presence, patience, and unconditional love.**

PART SEVEN: SPECIFIC RELATIONSHIPS

Chapter 14: If You Are...

While this book is written primarily for parents, it may have found its way to you through a different relationship. This chapter addresses the specific dynamics and opportunities that come with being a sibling, friend, or new partner of a man in a coercive control relationship. The core principles apply across all relationships, but each position has its own characteristics.

His Parent

If you are his parent, most of this book has been written with you in mind. This section summarises the key points and addresses some dynamics specific to the parent-child relationship.

Your Unique Position

As a parent, you have both advantages and disadvantages in this situation:

- **Deep history.** You knew him before her. You have decades of relationship that predates the abuse. For many parents, part of the pain here is specifically about watching a son who once seemed confident, capable, and independent become smaller inside himself. You are not only grieving your child; you may also be grieving the man you watched him become, and the way that man now seems to have been erased.

- **Unconditional bond.** The parent-child bond carries particular weight. Even when relationships are strained, most people retain a sense that parents are parents - that they will be there in ways others might not. This bond is harder for her to fully sever.

- **But also: parental authority triggers.** Your history includes the years when you had authority over him. Attempts to guide or protect him can trigger the adolescent impulse to assert independence. He may resist your input precisely because it comes from a parent.

- **And: easier to dismiss.** "My mother never liked any of my girlfriends." "My father always thinks he knows best." His partner can frame your concern as predictable parental overreach rather than legitimate observation.

Managing the Parent Role

The most effective parental stance is one that respects his adulthood while offering continued connection:

- **Offer, don't impose.** "I'm here if you need me" lands differently than "You need to listen to me." The first respects his autonomy; the second triggers resistance.

- **Be a parent, not a rescuer.** Your job is not to save him from his life choices. It is to remain present and connected while he navigates his own path. This distinction is crucial and difficult.

- **Mind your own history.** If your relationship with him has always been complicated, those complications don't disappear in crisis. Old patterns may resurface. Being aware of your own tendencies: toward control, toward worry, toward distance helps you avoid repeating them.

- **Coordinate with your partner.** If you are parenting together, alignment matters. Different approaches from mother and father can be exploited or can create confusion. Find a shared stance and support each other in maintaining it.

Mother Versus Father Dynamics

Mothers and fathers often experience and respond to this situation differently:

- **Mothers** may feel the situation more viscerally. The instinct to protect can be overwhelming. Mothers may also be more likely to be dismissed: "You're overreacting," "You're being emotional," "You never liked her." The gendered dismissal of maternal concern is a tool abusers can exploit.

- **Fathers** may struggle with the helplessness of the situation. The male instinct to fix, to act, to solve is thwarted by a problem that cannot be fixed through action. Fathers may also carry particular weight when speaking about relationship dynamics or may be less likely to be heard on emotional matters.

When the victim is their son, many fathers also feel an additional layer of shame and confusion: they may quietly question whether they "raised him wrong," whether his victimisation reflects on their own masculinity, or whether they should have seen the signs earlier. This self-blame can drive them toward more forceful interventions just when restraint is most needed.

Neither mother nor father has an inherently better position. What matters is that each parent manages their own tendencies and that parents work together rather than at cross purposes.

His Sibling

If you are his brother or sister, your position is different from a parent's in important ways. Sibling relationships carry their own dynamics, advantages, and challenges.

Your Unique Position

- **Peer relationship.** Unlike parents, siblings are peers. There is no inherent authority differential. This can make your input easier to receive. You're not telling him what to do from a position of parental authority; you're sharing perspective from someone who grew up alongside him.

- **Shared history.** You share childhood experiences, family context, and often a communication style shaped by growing up together. This shared language can create connection that outsiders cannot replicate.

- **Less threatening.** His partner may perceive siblings as less threatening than parents. Sibling relationships may be permitted more latitude, providing access that parents don't have.

- **But also: sibling history.** Sibling relationships carry their own baggage. Old rivalries, established roles, historical conflicts - these don't vanish. If you were always the "bossy older sister" or the "irresponsible younger brother," these frames may affect how your input is received.

Sibling Strategies

- **Maintain the relationship you had.** Whatever your sibling relationship was before (close confidants, occasional contact, something in between) try to maintain it. Sudden intensification of contact can feel suspicious or pressured. Continue being the sibling you've always been.

    Sibling activities. If you have activities you've traditionally done together: watching sports, playing games, particular rituals - continue them. These provide connection and normalcy without requiring heavy conversation.

- **Be a peer, not a parent.** Avoid falling into parental patterns: lecturing, warning, expressing disappointment. You're his sibling; act like one. Peers can express concern once and then let it go in ways parents sometimes cannot.

- **Coordinate with parents.** If your parents are also involved, some coordination is valuable. You don't need to be a unified front, but knowing what approaches have been tried and how he's responded helps everyone avoid repeating mistakes.

When Siblings Disagree About the Situation

In families with multiple siblings, not everyone may see the situation the same way. One sibling may be convinced of abuse while another thinks the family is overreacting. One may want to intervene directly while another advocates patience.

These disagreements can fracture family response. A sibling who doesn't see the problem may become a conduit for information to his partner, or may actively undermine other family members' efforts.

Where possible, have conversations within the family about what you're each observing and what approaches you're taking. Agreement may not be possible, but at minimum, understanding each other's positions helps prevent family conflict from making the situation worse.

His Friend

If you are his friend, you occupy a position with particular value. Friends are chosen rather than given by birth. Your presence in his life represents something that exists outside family obligation.

For many men, friendships are built more around shared activity than around emotional disclosure. That does not mean your role is minor. It means that simply staying in his orbit, doing ordinary things together, may be one of the safest ways for him to stay connected to a life outside the relationship.

Your Unique Position

- **Chosen relationship.** He chose you as a friend. This carries different weight than family relationships that exist by default. Your presence in his life reflects something about who he is and what he values.

- **Outside the family system.** You exist outside family dynamics that his partner may have mapped and is working to manipulate. You represent connection to an identity and a life that predates her.

- **But also: easier to cut.** Friendships are easier to sever than family relationships. If his partner decides you are a threat, eliminating your influence may be straightforward. Conflicts can be manufactured, your visits discouraged, your calls not returned until the friendship fades.

- **And: less information.** You may see him less frequently than family. You may have less context for how things have changed. Your baseline for "who he was" may be less detailed.

Friend Strategies

Men often disclose indirectly and slowly. A complaint about being tired at the pub, a half-joke about "being in trouble again," or a story that does not quite add up may be his way of testing whether it is safe to say more. Your job is not to interrogate those moments, but to respond in ways that signal you can handle the truth if he ever wants to share it.

- **Persist gently.** When he cancels plans, doesn't return calls, or seems to be fading away, don't take it personally and don't give up. Keep reaching out at reasonable intervals. The door should remain open from your side even when he seems to be closing it.

- **Create low-pressure opportunities.** Invitations should be easy to accept: casual, flexible, without pressure. "Want to grab coffee sometime?" is easier to say yes to than elaborate plans. Make it easy for him to maintain connection.

- **Include her when necessary.** If he can only see friends when she's present, accept her presence. Some connection is better than none. You can maintain friendship even with a chaperone.

- **Don't compete with her.** Making him choose between you and her is a losing proposition. She controls far more of his life than you do. Avoid situations that force choice.

- **One honest conversation, once.** If you have concerns, you can express them: once, clearly, and without repetition. "I've noticed some things that worry me. I don't know the full picture, but I want you to know I'm here if you ever want to talk." Then drop it. You've planted the seed; whether it grows is not in your control.

When Friends Don't See It

If you are reading this book because someone else has given it to you, a family member who is worried, you may be uncertain whether their concerns are valid. His family sees things you don't; you see things his family doesn't.

Consider what you've observed. Has he changed since the relationship began? Does he seem anxious about her reactions? Has his world contracted? Do you see him less? Does she dominate conversation when present?

You don't need to reach the same conclusions as his family to be a valuable presence in his life. Even if you are unsure whether this is "really abuse," you can still be the friend who does not disappear when things get strange. Men in coercive control relationships often lose friends to awkwardness and confusion rather than to conflict. Simply staying connected, remaining available, and being willing to listen matters regardless of how you interpret the situation.

His New Partner

If you have begun a relationship with a man who has left a coercive control relationship, you are entering a situation with particular complexity. Understanding what he has been through - and what recovery looks like - helps you support him while also protecting yourself.

What You Need to Understand

- **He is not fully recovered.** Regardless of how put-together he seems, leaving a coercive control relationship is the beginning of recovery, not the end. He may have trauma responses, trust issues, and patterns developed in the abusive relationship that will surface in your relationship.

- **His reactions may not be about you.** He may flinch at things that seem innocuous. He may have disproportionate responses to situations that remind him of the abuse. His nervous system has been recalibrated by years of hypervigilance, and it takes time to recalibrate again.

- **She may still be present.** Especially if children are involved, his ex-partner remains part of his life. You may encounter her manipulation, her attempts to disrupt his new relationships, her use of the children as leverage. This is not baggage he chose; it is reality he is navigating.

- **It is also likely that she has told a very different story** about the relationship to people around her, including people you may eventually meet. You may hear versions where she is the victim and he is the abuser. This is common in abusive dynamics and can make it harder to trust your own experience of him.

- **His family has been through something too.** His parents, siblings, and friends have watched someone they love suffer and have felt helpless to stop it. Their relationship with you may carry intensity born of relief that he is finally with someone healthy or wariness that this might be another problematic relationship.

Patterns to Watch For

Survivors of coercive control often carry patterns from the abusive relationship that can affect new relationships:

- **Fawning and people-pleasing.** He may be excessively focused on your needs, suppressing his own to avoid conflict. This can feel flattering initially: he's so attentive! But, it's not healthy for either of you. He needs to learn that it's safe to have needs and preferences.

- **Difficulty expressing needs.** After years of having his needs dismissed or punished, he may struggle to identify what he wants, let alone ask for it. Encourage him to express preferences and honour them when he does.

- **Over-explaining.** He may feel the need to justify everything. Where he was, what he was doing, why he made any decision. This is a habit developed when every action was scrutinised. Let him know he doesn't need to explain himself to you. For a man who has been repeatedly accused or suspected, offering long explanations can feel like a pre-emptive defence. He may not yet trust that "I went out with a mate" is enough.

- **Waiting for the other shoe to drop.** He may have difficulty trusting that good periods will last. In the abusive relationship, good times were followed by bad; he may be bracing for your warmth to turn into punishment.

- **Triggers.** Specific phrases, tones, situations, or dynamics may trigger trauma responses. These triggers may not be predictable and may surprise both of you.

Supporting His Recovery

- **Patience.** Recovery is not linear. He will have good periods and setbacks. Healing cannot be rushed or demanded.

- **Consistency.** Being predictable and reliable helps rebuild his capacity to trust. Say what you mean, follow through on commitments, and be who you say you are.

- **Space for his experience.** Let him talk about what happened when he needs to. Don't rush him past the processing. Avoid comparing your previous relationships to his - what he experienced was qualitatively different.

- **Acknowledge the language of abuse.** When the genders are reversed, people are more likely to question whether it "really counts" as abuse. If you can believe him, without minimising or rushing to silver linings, you offer something he may never have had before: a person who sees what happened and does not secretly hold it against him.

- **Encourage professional support.** You cannot be his therapist. Your relationship should not be organised around his healing. Encourage him to work with a professional, and make space for that work.

- **Maintain your own life.** It's easy to become absorbed in supporting his recovery. But you need your own friendships, interests, and support system. A healthy relationship requires two whole people, not a caretaker and a patient.

Protecting Yourself

Supporting a trauma survivor is demanding. You need to protect your own wellbeing:

- **Don't lose yourself.** Your needs matter. Your feelings matter. A relationship where you constantly subordinate yourself to his healing needs is not healthy. And ironically, it may replicate dynamics he needs to unlearn.

- **Set boundaries.** Understanding where his behaviour comes from doesn't mean accepting behaviour that harms you. Trauma is an explanation, not a permission slip. He still needs to treat you well.

- **Watch for unhealthy patterns.** Some survivors of abuse become abusive themselves. Some choose new partners with similar dynamics. If you find yourself being controlled, criticised, or manipulated, his history does not excuse it.

- **Get your own support.** Talking to a therapist, a support group for partners of trauma survivors, or trusted friends helps you process what you're experiencing and maintain perspective.

Building Something Healthy

The goal is not a relationship organised around his trauma but a healthy relationship between two adults. His past is part of who he is, and understanding it helps you support him. But it should not define the relationship.

Healthy relationships after abuse are absolutely possible. Many survivors go on to build loving, functional partnerships. The key is that recovery is ongoing, professional support is engaged, and both partners are committed to building something different from what came before.

You are not responsible for fixing him. You are responsible for being a good partner. Sometimes those overlap; sometimes they don't. Knowing the difference is essential.

A Professional Working With Him

If you are a therapist, counsellor, doctor, lawyer, or other professional working with a man you suspect may be in a coercive control relationship, your position carries both opportunity and responsibility.

Recognising the Signs

Coercive control in men presents differently than professionals often expect. Signs to watch for include:

- Anxiety or checking behaviour around phone calls from a partner
- Unexplained changes in presentation: weight loss, fatigue, withdrawal
- Excessive self-blame for relationship difficulties
- Describing partner behaviour that sounds controlling but is framed as reasonable
- Social isolation: reduction in friendships, family contact, outside activities
- Financial stress that seems inconsistent with income
- Partner who insists on attending appointments or knowing what was discussed
- Presenting issues that could be symptoms of abuse: anxiety, depression, substance use, stress-related physical complaints

Creating Safety to Disclose

Male victims are unlikely to volunteer that they are being abused. The barriers to disclosure: shame, minimisation, fear of not being believed are substantial.

Creating conditions where disclosure becomes possible includes:

- Asking directly about relationship dynamics, in private, without the partner present
- Using language that does not assume gender: "Do you feel safe at home?" rather than "Does she hit you?"

- Normalising male victimhood: acknowledging that men can be victims of controlling relationships

- Being prepared to hear answers that challenge assumptions

- Following up over time: disclosure may not happen in the first conversation

What Not to Do

- **Don't refer to couples therapy.** If coercive control is present, couples therapy can make things worse by giving the abuser new tools and a professional to manipulate.

- **Don't apply standard relationship advice.** "Communicate more" and "consider her perspective" are appropriate in healthy relationships but can reinforce abusive dynamics in coercive control situations.

- **Don't assume he's the perpetrator.** If he describes conflict or difficult dynamics, don't default to assuming he's the one causing problems. Men presenting with relationship difficulties deserve the same presumption of good faith as women.

- **Don't push disclosure before he's ready.** You can create space for disclosure without forcing it. He may need multiple conversations before he's ready to name what's happening.

Providing Appropriate Support

If he does disclose, appropriate professional support includes:

- Believing him and affirming that what he's experiencing is real and serious

- Providing information about coercive control that helps him understand the dynamics

- Connecting him with appropriate resources such as Stand Again

- Supporting his safety planning if he's considering leaving

- Respecting his timeline and autonomy. He may not be ready to leave

- Maintaining confidentiality to the extent your professional obligations allow

Your role is to support his process, not to direct it. He has been controlled enough; what he needs from professionals is expertise offered in ways that respect his autonomy.

KEY TAKEAWAY:

- **EACH RELATIONSHIP POSITION OFFERS DIFFERENT ADVANTAGES AND CHALLENGES.**

- **PARENTS CARRY DEEP HISTORY BUT MAY TRIGGER INDEPENDENCE RESISTANCE. SIBLINGS OFFER PEER RELATIONSHIPS WITHOUT AUTHORITY DYNAMICS.**

- **FRIENDS REPRESENT CHOSEN CONNECTION BUT ARE EASIER TO CUT.**

- **NEW PARTNERS ENTER A COMPLEX RECOVERY LANDSCAPE REQUIRING PATIENCE AND BOUNDARIES.**

- **PROFESSIONALS HAVE UNIQUE OPPORTUNITY TO RECOGNISE AND SUPPORT MALE VICTIMS WHO MAY DISCLOSE NOWHERE ELSE.**

- **THE CORE PRINCIPLES – PRESENCE, PATIENCE, UNCONDITIONAL ACCEPTANCE – APPLY ACROSS ALL RELATIONSHIPS, ADAPTED TO EACH POSITION'S PARTICULAR DYNAMICS.**

PART EIGHT: THE LONG VIEW

Chapter 15: Living With Uncertainty

You may be reading this book in the early days of recognising the problem, or you may be years into a situation that shows no signs of resolution. This final chapter addresses the long view: how to sustain yourself when the timeline is indefinite, how to find meaning when outcomes are uncertain, and how to live fully even when someone you love remains trapped.

The Reality of Timelines

When you first recognise that your son is in a coercive control relationship, you naturally imagine resolution. He will see the truth. He will leave. Things will return to normal. This hope is necessary; it sustains you through the early period of helplessness and fear.

But resolution may not come quickly. It may not come at all. The timelines for these situations vary enormously:

- **Some people leave within months** of family recognition that something is wrong. The external concern reaches them at a moment of internal readiness, and movement happens relatively quickly.

- **Some people leave after years.** The process of recognition and movement unfolds slowly, with many false starts and returns. Families wait through long periods of apparent stasis before anything shifts.

- **Some people leave only when external circumstances force it** The abuser leaves them, the abuser dies, legal intervention occurs. Their own agency in leaving never fully develops, but they end up out nonetheless.

- **Some people never leave.** They remain in the relationship until they die. Whether that death is from natural causes, from the accumulated toll of chronic stress, or in rare cases, from the abuser's violence.

You cannot know which timeline applies to your son. You cannot know whether the things you do will contribute to eventual exit or whether exit will never come. This uncertainty is perhaps the hardest thing about this situation. The not knowing, indefinitely.

If He Never Leaves

This possibility must be faced honestly. Some people remain in abusive relationships for their entire lives. Your son may be one of them.

What This Means

If he never leaves, the relationship you have with him will be permanently shaped by her presence. You will never have your son fully back. Family gatherings will always include her influence. Grandchildren, if there are any, will grow up in that household.

This does not mean your relationship with him is worthless or that your efforts have been wasted. Connection maintained under difficult circumstances is still connection. Love expressed within constraints is still love. The light you leave on may provide warmth even if he never walks through the door.

But it does mean accepting a reality that falls far short of what you wanted for him. It may also mean accepting that the world will never see what you see. To his colleagues, neighbours, or wider community, he may appear to be the problem: the withdrawn husband, the checked-out father, the man who "lets" his partner behave this way.

Part of the grief for families of male victims is knowing that his suffering will probably never be publicly recognised or honoured.

It means grieving the life he might have had, the relationship you might have enjoyed, the person he might have become in different circumstances.

Maintaining Relationship Despite Everything

If he is not going to leave, the question becomes: what relationship is possible within these constraints?

- **Accept the limitations.** You will not have the relationship you want. You will have the relationship that is possible. Fighting constantly against the limitations exhausts you without changing them.

- **Find the connection that exists.** Within whatever access you have: family events, phone calls, brief visits there is still connection. It may be mediated, monitored, and constrained, but it is real.

- **Maintain your presence.** Even if nothing seems to change, continuing to exist in his life matters. He knows you are there. That knowledge may provide something, even if you cannot see what.

- **Let go of the outcome.** If you are maintaining connection in order to eventually get him out, the ongoing failure to achieve that goal will destroy you. If you are maintaining connection because connection has value in itself, you can sustain it indefinitely.

The Particular Pain of Watching

Watching someone you love suffer, year after year, without being able to help, is its own kind of trauma. You are a witness to ongoing harm. You see the diminishment, the exhaustion, the suppression of the person he could be. And you can do nothing but watch.

This witnessing takes a toll. The helplessness is corrosive. The grief is chronic. The anger - at her, at him, at the situation, at yourself - cycles without resolution.

Managing this long-term requires the strategies discussed in Chapter 6: your own therapy, your own support system, your own life that is not consumed by his situation. You cannot watch indefinitely without those supports. The watching will destroy you.

Sustainable Hope

Hope is necessary. Without it, you cannot continue. But the wrong kind of hope (hope attached to specific outcomes and timelines) leads to cycles of expectation and crushing disappointment.

Attached Hope Versus Open Hope

Attached hope sounds like:

- "He'll realise what's happening by Christmas."
- "Once the baby comes, she'll calm down."
- "The therapist will help him see."
- "He can't possibly stay another year."

This kind of hope is tied to specific expectations. When the expectation fails (and it usually does) the hope crashes into despair. Then hope rebuilds around a new expectation, and the cycle continues.

Open hope sounds like:

- "Things can change."
- "People do leave these relationships."
- "I don't know what will happen or when."
- "I remain present for possibility."

This kind of hope holds open the possibility of change without predicting when or how. It can coexist with uncertainty indefinitely because it doesn't depend on specific outcomes materialising on specific schedules.

Practicing Open Hope

Moving from attached hope to open hope is a practice, not a decision. It requires catching yourself when expectations form and gently releasing them.

When you notice yourself thinking "maybe this will be the year," you can acknowledge the thought without investing in it. "I notice I'm hoping for change. Change is possible. I don't know if it will happen."

This practice has something in common with meditation: the repeated returning from attachment to presence. You will attach to outcomes; that is human. The practice is in noticing the attachment and releasing it, again and again.

Hope and Grief Together

Open hope can coexist with grief in ways that attached hope cannot. You can simultaneously grieve what is: his ongoing entrapment, your limited relationship, the suffering you witness while remaining open to the possibility that things could change.

In fact, grieving what is may be necessary for sustainable hope. If you are fighting against reality, insisting that things should be different, you exhaust yourself. Accepting what is (which includes grieving it) frees energy for the long presence that open hope requires.

Your Life Beyond This

Your son's situation is not your whole life. It cannot be, not if you are to survive this journey. Part of the long view is maintaining and building a life that exists beyond his crisis.

Permission to Live

You may feel guilty for experiencing joy while he suffers. A good day can feel like betrayal. Laughter, pleasure, engagement with life: these can feel wrong when someone you love is trapped.

But your suffering does not help him. Your refusal to enjoy life does not reduce his pain. If anything, your wellbeing supports your capacity to be present for him. Taking care of yourself is not abandonment; it is sustainability.

You have permission to live your life. To pursue your interests. To enjoy your relationships. To find meaning and satisfaction in work, hobbies, friendships, and experiences. None of this diminishes your love for him or your commitment to remaining present.

Your Other Relationships

His crisis can consume so much attention that other relationships suffer. Your partner, your other children, your friends - all of these relationships need tending too.

Make deliberate space for these relationships. Don't let every conversation revolve around his situation. Be present with the people in front of you, not constantly mentally elsewhere. Your other relationships are not distractions from the real concern; they are part of the life that sustains you through the concern.

Finding Meaning

Some people in this situation find meaning by channelling their experience into helping others. Support groups for parents of adults in abusive relationships, advocacy work, writing or speaking about the issue. These activities transform private pain into public contribution.

This is not for everyone, and it is not required. But if you find that helping others in similar situations gives your experience meaning, that can be a valuable part of your long-term sustainability.

Meaning can also be found in things entirely unrelated to his situation. A garden, a craft, a community, a practice - whatever provides you purpose and engagement. Your life has meaning beyond being his parent, and attending to those other sources of meaning is not neglect.

What You Have Done

If you have read this book and tried to apply it, you have done something significant. You have chosen to stay engaged with a painful situation rather than withdrawing. You have tried to understand dynamics that are confusing

and counterintuitive. You have worked to be helpful in circumstances where the right thing to do is unclear.

The Value of Presence

Simply being present: maintaining connection, leaving the light on, remaining available is not nothing. It is, in fact, substantial.

Your presence means he is not entirely alone. Even if he cannot fully access the relationship, he knows it exists. Even if he cannot come to you, he knows you are there. In a situation designed to make him feel that no one cares and no alternatives exist, your presence is evidence to the contrary.

When the victim is a man, that counter-evidence is even more precious. So much of the story he absorbs: from services, from media, sometimes even from professionals is that men are the danger, not the ones in danger. You become the quiet proof that at least one person sees him clearly and does not confuse his victimhood with failure or weakness.

This matters whether or not he ever leaves. It matters whether or not he consciously recognises it. The human need for connection is deep, and providing it (even in constrained form) is an act of love that has value in itself.

What You Cannot Control

You have done what you can do. The outcome is not in your hands.

Whether he leaves, when he leaves, how he leaves. These are not things you control. You have influenced the conditions. You have maintained connection. You have positioned yourself to matter if and when he's ready. But the actual movement must come from him.

This lack of control is maddening. Every instinct tells you to do more, try harder, find the key that unlocks the situation. But the key is not yours to find. He holds it, and he will use it or not according to his own internal process.

Accepting what you cannot control is not giving up. It is recognising reality. It is freeing yourself from responsibility for things that are not yours to determine. It is, paradoxically, what allows you to continue being present without being destroyed by the weight of impossible obligation.

Your Reality is Hard

You are reading this book because someone you love is suffering and you want to help. That impulse to move toward someone in pain, to offer what you have, to not look away - is beautiful. It is what makes family mean something.

The situation you are in is genuinely hard - there is no denying that. There are also no easy answers, no guaranteed strategies, no clear paths to resolution. You are navigating something that would be difficult for anyone, and you are doing it out of love – that matters.

Whether he leaves next week or never, whether your relationship flourishes or remains constrained, whether this story has a happy ending or an ambiguous one - what you have offered matters.

The love you have expressed matters.

The presence you have maintained matters.

You cannot swoop in and save him. But you can love him. And you have.

KEY TAKEAWAY:

- **THE LONG VIEW REQUIRES ACCEPTING UNCERTAINTY ABOUT TIMELINES AND OUTCOMES.**

- **HE MAY LEAVE QUICKLY, SLOWLY, OR NEVER. SUSTAINABLE HOPE – OPEN TO POSSIBILITY WITHOUT ATTACHMENT TO SPECIFIC OUTCOMES – ALLOWS YOU TO REMAIN PRESENT INDEFINITELY.**

- **YOUR LIFE BEYOND HIS SITUATION MUST BE MAINTAINED AND VALUED.**

- **WHAT YOU HAVE DONE - STAYING ENGAGED, REMAINING PRESENT, LEAVING THE LIGHT ON - MATTERS REGARDLESS OF OUTCOME.**

- **YOU CANNOT SAVE HIM, BUT YOU CAN LOVE HIM. AND THAT IS NOT NOTHING.**

Conclusion

Stand Again and all the resources we have developed, including The Blueprint of Family Violence Against Men, and the four stages of healing that sit alongside it, grew out of my own lived experience: the experience of men who could not find themselves in existing models, and of families who watched them disappear.

This book is one attempt to hand you a map, so you don't have to walk blind. It was written because families of male abuse victims have almost no resources designed specifically for them.

The challenges you face: the invisibility of his suffering, the systems that may not believe him, the particular ways male conditioning shapes his experience deserve acknowledgment and guidance.

The journey you are on is difficult. But you are not alone in it. Other families are maintaining the same vigil, leaving the same lights on, waiting for the same uncertain possibilities. There is a community of people who understand what you are going through, even if they are not visible to you.

It matters.

At time of writing, Stand Again is self-funded and sustained by the people it serves.

If you have found this book helpful **you can support Stand Again** by:

- Donating to Stand Again at www.standagain.com.au
- Following and sharing the Stand Again social media channels so more families can find their way to this map

Thank you for trying. Thank you for staying. Thank you for loving someone through circumstances that make love difficult.

And no matter how many times you have been knocked down. You can Stand Again.

APPENDIX

Appendix A: Quick Reference

This appendix provides at-a-glance summaries of key concepts from the book for quick reference.

Signs He May Be in a Coercive Control Relationship

Changes in him:

- Personality seems flattened, guarded, or different from who he was
- Reduced contact with family and friends
- Abandoned hobbies, interests, or friendships
- Constant checking of phone or anxiety about partner's reactions
- Excessive self-blame for relationship difficulties
- Physical signs: weight changes, fatigue, stress-related health issues
- Financial stress inconsistent with income

Relationship patterns:

- She accompanies him everywhere; he rarely appears alone
- He checks with her before making any plans
- Disproportionate defence of her against mild observations
- His explanations echo her language or seem rehearsed
- He speaks in "we" rather than "I"
- Last-minute cancellations of plans

The Five Stages at a Glance

Stage One: Deep in the System

He cannot see anything is wrong. Complete absorption in her framework. Your role: maintain warm, low-pressure connection. Do not criticise her or present evidence.

Stage Two: Cracks Forming

Moments of doubt are surfacing. He may ask questions or make small complaints. Your role: provide safe space for emerging doubts without pushing conclusions. Listen more than you speak.

Stage Three: Crisis Point

Something has happened that cannot be explained away. Acute distress. Your role: provide immediate practical support, calm presence, non-judgmental listening. Avoid "I told you so."

Stage Four: Early Exit

He has left but is not yet stable. Ambivalence and possible return. Your role: provide stability and practical support. Respect his pace. If he returns, keep the door open.

Stage Five: Reconstruction

Exit has stabilised. Long-term rebuilding begins. Your role: support his emerging identity. Expect the anger phase. Accept he will be changed by this experience.

Core Principles

- Leave the light on. Maintain warm, consistent presence regardless of response.

- Warmth over pressure. Every interaction should leave him feeling better about contact with you.

- His timeline, not yours. Movement must come from him when he is ready.

- Unconditional presence. Your love and availability do not depend on him leaving.

- Sustainable hope. Hold open possibility without attaching to specific outcomes or timelines.

What to Avoid

- Criticising her directly

- Presenting evidence of abuse before he's ready

- Ultimatums or forced choices

- Formal interventions

- Going behind his back

- "I told you so" when he reaches out

- Expecting immediate decisions or linear progress

- Punishing him if he returns to her

Appendix B: Resources

Resources specifically for male victims and their families remain limited, but the following may be helpful. Availability and contact details may change; verify current information before relying on these services.

Australia

For Male Victims

Stand Again

Web: standagain.com.au

Education & support specifically for male victims of coercive control.

Men's Referral Service

Phone: 1300 766 491 Web: ntv.org.au

Support and referrals for men affected by family violence, including male victims.

One in Three Campaign

Web: oneinthree.com.au

Information and advocacy for male victims of family violence.

General Family Violence Services

1800RESPECT

Phone: 1800 737 732 Web: 1800respect.org.au

National sexual assault, domestic and family violence counselling service.

Lifeline

Phone: 13 11 14 24/7

Crisis support and suicide prevention.

Legal

Family Relationships Advice Line

Phone: 1800 050 321

Information about family law and separation.

United Kingdom

ManKind Initiative

Web: mankind.org.uk

Support for male victims of domestic abuse.

Men's Advice Line

Phone: 0808 801 0327 Web: mensadviceline.org.uk

Advice and support for men experiencing domestic violence.

United States

National Domestic Violence Hotline

Phone: 1-800-799-7233 Web: thehotline.org

Support for all victims of domestic violence.

DAHMW (Domestic Abuse Helpline for Men and Women)

Phone: 1-888-743-5754

Support specifically inclusive of male victims.

For Family Members

Formal support groups specifically for families of male abuse victims are rare. Consider:

- Online communities for parents of adults in abusive relationships (search for support groups; these exist on various platforms)
- Al-Anon or similar groups (while focused on addiction, the dynamics of loving someone you cannot control have significant overlap)
- Individual therapy with a practitioner who understands coercive control dynamics

Finding Professional Support

When seeking therapists or counsellors, whether for him or for yourself, look for:

- Experience with domestic violence, coercive control, or intimate partner abuse
- Understanding that men can be victims
- Trauma-informed approach
- Willingness to work individually rather than defaulting to couples therapy

Interview potential therapists about their experience with these dynamics before committing. A therapist who does not understand coercive control may inadvertently cause harm.

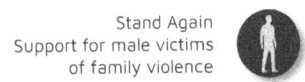

Acknowledgments

This book exists because of the families who shared their experiences: the confusion, the helplessness, the grief, and the hope that persists despite everything. Their willingness to talk about what they were going through, often without any existing language for it, made it possible to write something that might help others.

It exists because of the male survivors who broke their silence and described what they experienced from the inside. The psychological architecture of coercive control, the particular ways it exploits masculine conditioning, the long road to recovery. Their courage in speaking makes it possible for others to be seen.

It exists because of the professionals: therapists, advocates, researchers, who have worked to understand these dynamics and to develop approaches that actually help. Their insights inform every chapter.

And it exists because of the growing recognition that domestic abuse affects people of all genders, that male victims deserve support, and that the families who love them deserve guidance. The conversation is changing, slowly. This book is a contribution to that change.

To everyone who shared their story, their expertise, or their encouragement: thank you.

www.ingramcontent.com/pod-product-compliance
Lightning Source LLC
Chambersburg PA
CBHW061123070526
44583CB00028B/3366